Why Believe?

Why Believe?

John Cottingham

continuum

Continuum International Publishing Group
The Tower Building, 11 York Road, London SE1 7NX
80 Maiden Lane, Suite 704, New York NY 10038

www.continuumbooks.com

First published 2009
Paperback edition published 2011

British Library Cataloguing-in-Publication Data
A catalogue record for this book is available from the British Library.

ISBN 978-0-8624-9636-2 (hardback)
     978-1-4411-4305-1 (paperback)

Typeset by Kenneth Burnley, Wirral, Cheshire
Printed and bound in India

For LWC and FJW

Contents

Foreword

Writing about religious belief is a perilous undertaking. There are so many people one risks offending. In the first place, there is the problem of the implied audience. I have endeavoured to write for believers as well as non-believers, and I know the issues are ones about which, in both camps, there are very strong feelings. Disagreement can rapidly turn to anger when the allegiances involved go to the heart of who one is and how one lives; and (as I have discovered in previous forays in this area) attempts to be tactful and non-partisan can provoke even more annoyance. Nevertheless, I do sincerely believe that religion is not some special battleground, lying outside the citadel of normal human experience and culture, but that the religious outlook (or its absence) is something deeply inter-twined with ordinary human concerns which we all share. So however fierce the schisms and factions, there is, in the end, a vast amount of common ground, and it is here, I believe, that fruitful discussion can occur. One also needs to remember that, notwithstanding the ranks of dogmatists on either side, there are many people who are genuinely undecided about whether they could ever be religious believers; and these readers too, perhaps especially these readers, are among those I should like to reach.

On the academic front, questions about belief in God lie at the interface between philosophy and theology, yet philosophers and theologians come to the subject with very different expectations. The prevailing tide of contemporary analytic philosophy tends to be strongly naturalistic, and any reference to the supernatural will cause many readers to switch off. One task of the believing philosopher, as I see it, is to try to open the minds of secular readers to the immense riches of the religious culture that has come down to us – a culture whose texture used to be deeply woven into the conceptual fabric of Western thought, but which in many cases has scarcely touched the education or upbringing of younger generation intellectuals, at least in Western Europe. (In North America, the problem is rather different, not so much of ignorance of religious culture, but of a marked polarization between its supporters and its critics.) At all events, even at the risk of the 'switch-off effect', I have provided many scriptural references, in the hope that at least something of the interest of these texts to anyone concerned with the human predicament will emerge, irrespective of religious allegiance or its absence. In the process, however, there is of course the corresponding danger that theologians, excessively familiar with these materials, will find the references laboured and redundant. All I can say is that I have tried to strike a balance which will, I hope, keep the majority of readers on board, at least for a while.

In part, this book is unashamedly a piece of advocacy, and the style may in a few places perhaps be more rhetorical or emotionally laden than is normally considered acceptable in academic discourse. I make no apology for the advocacy, since in reality even the most seemingly austere and 'detached' philosophical writing is often driven by a passionate desire to convince, and often the materials commonly marshalled merely as 'examples' or 'illustrations' turn out to pack a considerable emotional punch, or to function as powerful intuition pumps. But in any case, I have always had misgivings about the current philosophical fashion for affecting a detached and impersonal style of discourse – something wholly appropriate for natural science, but radically unsuited for a subject which in my view really only has a proper rationale, and a viable future, if it remains, in the phrase of Bernard Williams, a 'humanistic discipline'.[1]

Although my allegiances will be abundantly clear by the end of the book, I have tried not to adopt too partisan a tone, and have endeavoured to raise the issues involved in my theme in a way that will not alienate those who do not share my particular belief-system. In previous writing I have perhaps overdone this 'non-partisan' strategy, and talked rather generally of 'religious belief', without acknowledging that this label covers an enormous variety of systems, some of which are no doubt much more problematic than others. In the present book, I have often referred much more explicitly to Christian beliefs and practices; but this is not from any exclusivist principles, but in part because that is the culture in which I was raised, and

---

[1] Bernard Williams, 'Philosophy as a Humanistic Discipline' [2000].

it is better to work with materials one is familiar with. I believe however that it is possible to advocate a particular path without presuming to pass judgement upon other paths; and in the case of the three Abrahamic faiths at least, their histories, and the structures of their spirituality, are so deeply intertwined that the fiercer forms of exclusivism would end up being incoherent or self-destructive.

As with most of my writing, I have tried throughout to be as accessible as possible. This is partly because I do not think philosophy needs to be full of technical jargon in order to do its job properly, and partly because I do not think an argument is necessarily better if every thesis is hedged in with fearsome elaborations and qualifications. Often the result of such hyperdefensiveness can be writing that no one would willingly wade through unless their livelihood depended on it, or unless infected by the prevailing academicism that mistakes indigestibility for rigour. The opposite vice, of course, is oversimplification, and I am all too aware that many of the issues broached here demand a far more extended treatment than I have been able to afford them in such a comparatively slim volume; but I have tried nevertheless to achieve as much clarity and precision as the space and the subject matter allow.

Some particular professional debts are recorded in the Acknowledgements, but it is several more personal debts that have been crucial in shaping the outlook without which this book could not have been written. Foremost amongst these has been the influence of my immediate family. To its two most recent members, both born during the final months of writing, this book is dedicated, with love.

John Cottingham
Berkshire, England
March 2009

Acknowledgements

Part of Chapter 2 was delivered at a colloquium in honour of Gerry Hughes at Heythrop College, University of London, in December 2008; part of Chapter 3 was originally presented at a conference in honour of Herman de Dijn at the Philosophy Department of the Katholieke Universiteit Leuven, Belgium, in October 2008; part of Chapter 5 was presented at a conference on 'The Emotions in Ethics and Religion' at the University of Zurich in March 2008, and again at Claremont Graduate University, California in April 2009; and parts of Chapters 5 and 6 were included in a lecture given at the Ian Ramsay Centre for Science and Religion at Oxford University in February 2008. I am grateful to participants at all these events for helpful comments. In a number of places in the book I have drawn on material from previously published articles, and I am grateful to the publishers and editors for permission to include it here. The beginning of Chapter 6 makes use of one section from my paper 'The Lessons of Life: Wittgenstein, Religion and Analytic Philosophy', in J. Hyman and H.-J. Glock (eds), *Wittgenstein and Twentieth-Century Analytic Philosophy: Essays in Honour of P. M. S. Hacker* (Oxford: Oxford University Press, 2009), pp. 203–27; and part of Chapter 7 makes use of a portion of my article 'What Difference Does It Make? The Nature and Significance of Theistic Belief', in *Ratio* Vol. XIX, No. 4 (December 2006), pp. 401–20. I owe a debt of gratitude to many colleagues and friends who have enriched my understanding of the topics discussed here, especially to Douglas Hedley, Tim Mawson, Mark Wynn, Chris Hamilton and David Leal at a London-based Theology discussion group, and to the members of an Oxford-based Philosophy of Religion discussion group including Brian Leftow, Richard Swinburne, Roger Trigg and John Bishop. Finally, I am most grateful to Robin Baird-Smith at Continuum for encouraging me to undertake this project.

Chapter 1

Belief and its Benefits

The Word of Life is offered to a man, and on its being offered, he has Faith in it. Why? . . . Because he has a love for it, his love being strong, though the testimony is weak.

John Henry Newman[1]

1. How believing affects living

As part of a television broadcast entitled *The Genius of Charles Darwin*, the distinguished biologist and militant atheist Richard Dawkins was filmed taking a group of secondary-school children to a beach in Dorset where fossils were to be found that supported Darwin's theory of evolution. After showing them the evidence, he turned to them triumphantly and said: 'There now! Do you still believe in God?' Most were too deferential to challenge him directly, but some insisted that they would continue to pray.[2] Dawkins's assumption appeared to be that their religious

---

[1] John Henry Newman, *Sermons, Chiefly on the Theory of Religious Belief* [1826–1843], p. 195.
[2] *The Genius of Charles Darwin*, broadcast on Channel 4 (UK), 4 August 2008.

beliefs were the result of unthinking acceptance of what they had imbibed in early childhood, namely a naïve supernaturalist account of how life on earth had developed. But the students, perhaps with more insight than their eminent inquisitor, did not appear to feel that their religious commitments stood or fell with the truth or otherwise of Darwinian theory. Praying was, admittedly, something they had been taught to do in their early years, but it was something for which, as emerging young adults, many of them still felt a strong need. And neither the scientific questions about the development of life raised by Dawkins, nor the undoubted fact of Darwin's scientific genius, seemed, for them, to have much bearing on that.

There are grounds (which Dawkins, to his credit, elsewhere acknowledges)[3] for saying that religious impulses – to prayer and worship, for example – are deeply rooted in the life of our species. For whatever reason, the overwhelming majority of human beings in the course of our history to date, have felt a strong need for such activities. They need to lead their lives in faith, in hope, and in trust. Of course, trust can sometimes be misplaced. But human beings are not in the position of exalted judges sitting on the dais and being able to insist on exact evidence to warrant each of our life's commitments and actions. We are, on the contrary, *dependent* beings – 'dependent rational animals', in Alasdair MacIntyre's phrase[4] – caught up in a complicated nexus of demands and circumstances which we did not create, and which, whether we like it or not, determine the

---

[3] R. Dawkins, *The God Delusion*, Ch. 5.
[4] A. MacIntyre, *Dependent Rational Animals*.

conditions under which we have to conduct our lives. There is much even in our ordinary day-to-day existence that we inevitably have to take on trust; otherwise we would be paralysed with indecision, unable to achieve any kind of progress in our ordinary plans and projects.

That sense of dependence is surely one of the hallmarks of our human nature. Because our power to control our environment, and even the workings of our own bodies, has vastly increased with the growth of modern science, we may tend to ignore or gloss over the pervasive dependency of the human condition. Indeed, we may even indulge in a dream of autonomy and self-sufficiency, thinking that we are somehow completely 'in charge' of reality, or that we can totally control the conditions for our own fulfilment. Some may feel there is nothing wrong with this; but autonomy, in fact, can mean two things, one valuable, the other highly dubious. We certainly can, and should, aim to lead our lives without threat of interference or oppression – whether the external tyranny that comes from unwarranted political domination, or the internal tyranny that comes from disordered or confused desires, or lack of maturity and self-awareness. To wish to be free of these things is to aspire to a legitimate and benign autonomy. But there is a second, more suspect idea of autonomy, which involves the fantasy that we can somehow create our own values by some kind of godlike act of will – as if life were a 'blank slate' on which we can write any agenda we choose. Friedrich Nietzsche, proclaiming the 'death of God', envisaged a 'new philosopher' with a spirit 'strong enough to revalue and invert eternal values'.[5] But such a notion seems to involve a radical confusion. I cannot make something valuable by choosing or willing it (as if I could make coal nutritious by deciding to eat it); indeed, this idea precisely puts the cart before the horse, since in truth my choices or acts of will can be worthwhile only in so far as their objects already have independent value.

Whether or not there is a God, human beings did not create themselves – perhaps an obvious but nevertheless a salutary truth.[6] We are the products of an amazing (perhaps even ultimately mysterious) array of causes which operated long before we came on the scene and will continue to operate long after we are gone. That alone is enough to produce a sense of vertigo, of amazement, as we contemplate our own fragility and seeming insignificance against the infinite backdrop of time and space – the 'eternal silence of those infinite spaces' that terrified Pascal.[7] Yet so far from accepting, as the twentieth-century existentialists did, that our lives are absurd, or that we are free to invent any values we choose, many, perhaps most, human beings are drawn in an opposite direction. As we struggle through life, we seem compelled to acknowledge, sooner or later, that our human good, our flourishing and fulfilment, depends on orienting ourselves towards values that we did not

---

[5] Friedrich Nietzsche, *Beyond Good and Evil* [1886], §203.

[6] Compare the Psalmist: 'It is He who hath made us, and not we ourselves', Psalm 100 [99]:3. In references to the Psalms, the numbering given first is that of the Hebrew Bible (which is followed in the King James 'authorized version' and the Book of Common Prayer). The numbering supplied afterwards in square brackets is that of the Septuagint (Greek) and Vulgate (Latin) texts.

[7] Pascal, *Pensées* [1670], No. 206.

create. Love, compassion, mercy, truth, justice, courage, endurance, fidelity – all belong to a core of key virtues that all the world's great religions (and the secular cultures that have emerged from them) recognize, and which command our allegiance whether we like it or not. We may try to go against them, to live our lives without reference to them, but such attempts are always, in the end, self-defeating and productive of misery and frustration rather than human flourishing.

These facts are already, if we think about them, very striking and important ones. We are dependent and vulnerable creatures, who need, for our fulfilment, to orient ourselves towards certain enduring values. If we reflect on this, and couple it with an awareness of the obvious fact of our human weakness, and the notorious difficulty humans experience in steadfastly pursuing the good they aspire to, then one is struck by the extent to which religious belief offers a *home* for our aspirations. Theism, in its traditional form found in the three great Abrahamic faiths, involves the idea of a *match* between our aspirations and our ultimate destiny. On this picture, the creative power that ultimately shaped us is itself the source of the values we find ourselves constrained to acknowledge, and has made our nature such that we can find true fulfilment only in seeking those values. In the much-quoted words of St Augustine, 'You have made us for yourself and our heart is restless until it finds repose in you.'[8] The natural response to this – to acknowledge that creative source of goodness with joy, and to turn towards

---

[8] Augustine, *Confessions* [*c.* 398], Book I, Ch. 1.

it for strength in our struggle – is so basic that it presents itself
to the believer as a fundamental and necessary way of going
through life. It is not a matter of scientific hypotheses about the
precise macro- or micro-mechanisms that formed our planet
or our species, but rather a *necessary impulse of trust*, something that, as William Wordsworth conveyed in his poetry,
stems from moments of vivid awareness of the beauty and
goodness of the world and our place within it. It is an impulse
so deep that we feel that neither abstract intellectual speculation, nor the drudgery or pain of our routine existence,

> Shall e'er prevail against us, or disturb
> Our cheerful faith that all which we behold
> Is full of blessings.[9]

Few have been more eloquent advocates of the benefits of faith:
the uplifting sense of openness to beauty and goodness, and the
trust that our best and deepest aspirations in life are not arbitrary flailings around in the dark, but are part of the quest for
'God, who is our home'.[10] To describe God as our 'home' is to
conceive of him as the ultimate source from which we come
and the point of return to which our restlessness drives us – the
final end where our true peace lies. Of course, the cold light of
reason *may* compel us to turn our back on all this – that is a

9 William Wordsworth, 'Lines Written a Few Miles Above Tintern Abbey'
[1798], lines 135–6.

10 Wordsworth, 'Ode: Intimations of Immortality from Recollections of Early
Childhood' [1807], lines 64–5.

question we have not yet started to consider. But we need to be aware of what it is we would be rejecting.

2. How believing works

In moments of personal crisis – illness, bereavement, acute anxiety – one sometimes hears people utter phrases like 'I *wish* I could believe in God.' In saying this, the unbeliever is implicitly acknowledging that religious belief might bring certain benefits – comfort, perhaps, or consolation, or a sense of security or hope. But saying 'I wish I could' logically implies 'but unfortunately I can't'. There may be benefits; the benefits may even be readily acknowledged; but that is not enough to turn the non-believer into a believer.

Sometimes, of course, thinking about the benefits of doing something is quite enough to push people in a certain direction. 'Why should I go on holiday?' Because you are jaded and need time off to relax. 'Why go to the gym?' Because exercise is good for the health and will make you feel better. Focusing on such benefits can be, and often is, persuasive in getting someone to change their mind. But religious belief, however beneficial it may be for the believer, doesn't seem to work like that. I can book a holiday by picking up the phone; I can join a gym by clicking on the internet. But I can't, it seems, decide to be a believer, just like that.

Why not? There are many examples of beliefs I am incapable of forming at will, however much I might want to.[11] When I

---

[11] Bernard Williams, 'Deciding to Believe', in *Problems of the Self*, Ch. 9.

pick up the cup of green tea on my desk, and find it has gone cold, I can't decide to believe it is still warm. Once I take a sip of the disappointingly cool liquid, the belief that it has gone cold forms itself automatically in my mind – however much I might *like* to believe that it's still warm, or however pleasant it might be for me to think I do not to have to get up and put the kettle on again. Believing generally appears to be something that occurs involuntarily, like blushing or contracting the pupils of one's eyes. Suppose someone offers me a thousand pounds if I blush within five seconds, or free transport for life if I can contract the pupils of my eyes. However big the benefits, I may be forced to say, 'Sorry, I just can't do it.'

On reflection, though, I might find a way to make myself blush. I may not be able to do it 'just like that', but I might adopt an indirect technique – for example, thinking about a particularly embarrassing and humiliating episode in my life. This might make me blush, and I could then claim the money. So even if blushing is, in itself, something involuntary, it can *indirectly* be brought under voluntary control. And the same goes for contracting the pupils of my eyes. As every medical student knows, this is a very basic, utterly involuntary reflex; so I can't decide to do it just like that. But I can make it happen, for example by turning my head and looking at a bright light.

Blaise Pascal, an eminent mathematician and scientist as well as a devout Christian, observed in the seventeenth century that there may be indirect ways to bring it about that one becomes a religious believer. He suggested, for example, that going regularly to Mass might have the desired effect. Was he advocating a kind of self-manipulation or self-hypnosis?

I don't think so. His point was that becoming a believer is in part an emotional, not just an intellectual matter. 'You must realize', he said, 'that your inability to believe comes from your *passions*.'[12] Engaging in certain moving acts of worship (singing hymns perhaps, chanting psalms, directing one's thoughts to higher things as the incense drifts upwards) might have the effect of softening the heart, changing one's feelings, and so opening oneself to possibilities that had seemed closed before. So although one may not be able to decide to become a believer 'just like that', it might be possible to adopt an indirect strategy, like starting to attend church services, thereby embarking on a course of conduct that might lead, at the end of the road, to belief, or to faith. And if there really are great benefits in being a believer, then why not go ahead and give it a try? In the words of Pascal, 'What have you got to lose?'

At this point, some people may be outraged by the way the discussion is going. We seem to have embarked on a discussion of whether it might be possible to get oneself to believe, in order to gain the benefits of being a believer. But even if there are such benefits (and that is something many might dispute), isn't there something corrupt about the whole idea of looking at the *advantages* of believing something? A belief may be very soothing, comforting, reassuring, even good for the health, but surely that doesn't make it *true*? Compare the question 'Why believe in God?' with such questions as 'Why believe there is life

---

12 Pascal, *Pensées*, No. 418.

on other worlds?', or 'Why believe the food on your plate is wholesome?' In asking these latter questions we are clearly not inquiring whether it might be nice or comforting, or convenient, or reassuring to believe these things, but whether they are *true*. And similarly, in the religious case, our critic might object, we should surely not be talking about the *benefits* of belief, but the *evidence* or *justification* for belief.

I certainly do not want to sidestep the question of truth and of evidence – indeed it will be a central topic in the rest of this chapter and in subsequent chapters. But I do not think we should entirely dismiss the question of benefits. There are many things in my life I hold on to because I need to: because my life would fall apart if I ceased to trust in them. To get to work, I need to believe my car will not explode when I switch on the ignition, even though I have not conducted an exhaustive safety check on the wiring system. To engage in the ordinary necessary activities of life, such as eating, I need to trust in the nutritional value of certain foods, even though, as David Hume observed, there is no strict logical guarantee that the bread that nourished me at lunchtime will not poison me at suppertime.[13] The philosopher René Descartes, for all his obsession with the need for knowledge based on 'clearly and distinctly' perceived truths, was quick to acknowledge that in matters concerning the conduct of life, we often need to take decisions on the basis of very imperfect knowledge; and it would be ridiculous (and dangerous) to insist on waiting for

---

[13] David Hume, *An Enquiry concerning Human Understanding* [1748], Sectn IV, part 2.

completely clear evidence before proceeding.[14] If the plane I am flying on has to ditch in the sea, it would be silly to wait for a technical report on the condition of my lifejacket before donning it. So if the benefits associated with ordinary physical welfare require us to place a considerable measure of trust in matters where we have no guarantee of truth, why should it not be reasonable to have the same sort of trust when it comes to the benefits associated with our spiritual welfare?

You may reply that the two cases are different. Granted, I may not be able to prove my car has not been wired to explode, or my bread not been poisoned; but (unless I am a prominent terrorist target) common sense and previous experience make it perfectly reasonable to assume my car and my supper have not been tampered with. I trust my food and my means of transport not just because it's convenient and comforting and beneficial for me to do so, but also because there is at least some prior evidence that my trust is well founded. Yet in the religious case, by contrast, many people would say the evidence for reasonable belief is simply lacking. So in asking 'Why believe?', we surely cannot avoid tackling the question of evidence.

3. Belief and human sensibilities

The term 'evidence' often conjures up images of the courtroom, or the laboratory, and if we have these contexts in mind then it seems clear that what are needed are the tools of detached

---

14 René Descartes, *Discourse on the Method* [1637], Part III.

rational scrutiny and careful quantitative measurement. But there is much else in human experience that is not susceptible of this kind of assessment, or at least not entirely so. The kind of experience already mentioned, of which Wordsworth spoke in his poetry, provides a case in point. Not everyone may have a taste for the poetic voice in which Wordsworth expressed his ecstatic joy in the sublime beauty of the natural world, but hardly anyone could honestly say that they have never been profoundly moved by the wonders of nature. For Wordsworth, moreover, this was not just an 'aesthetic' matter, or a purely perceptual phenomenon; his experience could not be abstracted from its deeper moral meaning – the 'sense sublime of something far more deeply interfused' – which he glimpsed behind it.[15] Not everyone, to be sure, experiences the world around us in the same way. But I conjecture that very few people, if forced to be sincere, could honestly repudiate the twofold sense of 'awe' of which the philosopher Immanuel Kant spoke: the wonder at the vast splendour of the starry universe we inhabit, and the wonder at the strange compelling power of the moral values that call forth our allegiance.[16]

Now of course it *may* be possible to give deflationary explanations of these responses: perhaps wonder at nature is just some kind of evolutionary by-product of a capacity for being 'taken aback' by something that exceeds our comprehension – a capacity that might be useful for security and survival. And perhaps the resounding call of morality is just some kind of

---

[15] Wordsworth, 'Tintern Abbey', line 124.
[16] Immanuel Kant, *Critique of Practical Reason* [1788], conclusion.

illusion – for example, the voice of the Freudian superego produced by childhood conditioning, without any genuine objective authority or normative power behind it. But if it turns out that such deflationary accounts cannot wholly succeed in explaining them away, then the human responses we are discussing cannot simply be brushed aside as an irrelevance, or a distraction from the sober questions of evidence and justification. If we find ourselves in honesty compelled to acknowledge the power and apparent authenticity of such basic human responses, then they cannot just be swept aside as some kind of irrelevant emotional 'noise', but themselves need somehow to be fitted into our overall picture of the world and our place within it. They are, in short, a legitimate part of the phenomena to be considered, in any responsible approach to the question, 'Why believe?'

Nothing more distorts the mindset of the typical modern thinker than the unspoken assumption that only quantifiable, scientifically measurable aspects of things can count as genuine constituents of reality. Even a philosopher as brilliant as Bertrand Russell was tempted to say – absurdly – that tables and chairs are not 'really' solid, on the spurious grounds that they are made up of atoms that are largely comprised of gaps (the empty space between protons and electrons).[17] The truth, of course, is that the table I write on is really and genuinely solid; this is quite compatible with its being composed of arrangements of atoms which are not themselves solid. *Both* the commonsense, observable, macro-properties, *and* the

---

17 Bertrand Russell, *Problems of Philosophy* [1912], Ch. 1.

scientifically discovered micro-properties, are perfectly genuine, and it is a philosophical mistake to privilege either by saying one is more 'real' than the other.

Back in the seventeenth century, philosophers like Descartes and Locke divided reality into the objective, quantifiable phenomena studied by science, on the one hand, and the subjective 'ideas' (such as those of colour, heat, taste, smell, and so on), which they assigned to the separate mental domain of consciousness – the immaterial realm of minds or souls. Such a dualist view of reality made no bones about bracketing off the realm of human experience as an inner domain, wholly distinct from the objective natural world studied by science. But now that such dualism has been generally abandoned by modern science, our contemporary naturalistic scientists and philosophers face a problem: they cannot any longer separate off human experience and assign it to a mysterious immaterial realm, since on their own view of reality it must, in principle, be part of the total set of natural events that it is science's job to understand and explain. Once that is granted, the modern naturalistic philosopher or scientist cannot any longer dismiss our human aesthetic and moral and indeed religious impulses as belonging to the immaterial world of souls, and so irrelevant to science. Such impulses must be acknowledged as part of reality – *part of the evidence* that any responsible inquirer, however 'cold' and 'rational', is obliged to take into account.

The upshot is that it is incoherent for the modern inquirer to treat the question of the justification for religious belief in such a way as to exclude our human responses of vulnerability and dependence, of awe and wonder, of moral and spiritual awareness, as if they were irrelevant. They are, on any showing, *part of what we are*, part of our characteristic humanity. Such sensibilities, such yearnings, exist: that is certain. And that in itself has some considerable significance.

A natural yearning, implanted deep within us, may of course be vain, or fruitless, or have no object that can satisfy it; but that would be a tragic and ironic – perhaps even an absurdist – account of the human predicament. Such a view is possible – indeed it was eloquently articulated by philosophers such as Jean-Paul Sartre and Albert Camus. The image of the human condition that Camus left us with is that of Sisyphus, the 'true hero of the absurd', defiantly accepting his condemnation to a pointless and repetitive task with no value or purpose to redeem it.[18] But the very structure of the story, the very labelling of his plight as 'absurd', implies a deep yearning for something more. And it is precisely those yearnings that seem to feel an answering response via the kinds of joyful experience of which Wordsworth and many others have so eloquently spoken. To be sure, the fact that something would comfort our yearnings does not entail its truth; and, conversely, the fact that something is unpalatable and uncomfortable does not make it false. But equally, the cool and rational philosopher, the dispassionate and clear-eyed scientist, must be committed above all to intellectual integrity, or else he or she is nothing. And intellectual integrity requires that we do not ignore our deepest

---

[18] Albert Camus, *The Myth of Sisyphus* [1942], final chapter.

sensibilities and impulses. Either they must be explained away as distortions or seductive illusions, or their authenticity as possible pointers to something real must be acknowledged. There is no middle ground.

4. Belief and integrity

'Give me, O Lord, an undivided heart', asks the Psalmist.[19] Integrity is perhaps the hardest virtue to achieve – not merely making sure that one is steadfast in sticking to one's principles (or examining them critically when honesty so requires), but striving to make sure that all parts of our outlook fit together, that there are no hidden projections or self-deceptions distorting our attitudes, and that all our beliefs are held sincerely and responsibly. Religious belief, or its lack, is something that touches our integrity as or more deeply than any other aspect of our outlook. It goes to the heart of who we are, what we take ourselves to be doing with our lives, and how we locate ourselves in relation to others.

Yet it is extraordinarily easy to allow our integrity to be compromised by preconceived opinions – prejudices that occupy our thinking so pervasively that they become the 'default' assumptions informing what count as feasible systems of belief. It takes a genuine effort for many people to bring themselves to take an open-minded look at the possibility of religious belief, given the vast amounts that have been written over the last hundred years or more about the supposed 'difficulties' of a theistic outlook in the modern world. Science, we are told, has

---

[19] Psalm 86 [85]:11.

'disenchanted' the world; the Enlightenment has exiled religion from the domain of knowledge; Darwinism has made supernatural explanations of the world redundant; psychoanalytic theory has exposed religious impulses as infantile. For over a century the 'melancholy, long, withdrawing roar' of the sea of faith has been increasingly accepted as the unquestioned premise of inquiry among very many Western intellectuals. The oft-quoted phrase is from the third stanza of Matthew Arnold's 'Dover Beach' [*c.* 1851]:

> The Sea of Faith
> Was once, too, at the full, and round earth's shore
> Lay like the folds of a bright girdle furl'd.
> But now I only hear
> Its melancholy, long, withdrawing roar,
> Retreating, to the breath
> Of the night-wind, down the vast edges drear
> And naked shingles of the world.[20]

But what was once a piece of Victorian nostalgia for a faith that seemed to be ebbing away has now become for many an almost reflex refusal to consider religious belief as a live option. Conformity plays its part here. Academics are as susceptible to group pressure as anyone else, however much they may pride

---

20 Over a century later, Don Cupitt's *The Sea of Faith* [1984] suggested that the time had come to relinquish faith in a real objective God; the book led to the foundation of the 'Sea of Faith' movement, composed of clergy and others who openly espoused an anti-realist view of God (holding that God has no existence independent of human thinking and culture).

themselves as disinterested seekers after truth, and most university disciplines today operate within frameworks that are just as rigidly secular now as they would have been uncompromisingly theistic in the Middle Ages. But each individual who aims for integrity of outlook will sooner or later feel the need to delve behind the 'official' stance that they have almost imperceptibly been led to adopt, and ask themselves whether their own deepest responses, in their ordinary, non-professional lives, are actually consistent with the system of belief – in this case contemporary naturalistic secularism – to which they and their colleagues formally subscribe.

I am not here suggesting that academics are being intimidated into pretending to conform to the prevailing atheistical framework when privately they have doubts. That may no doubt sometimes happen, as the converse surely did in a previous 'age of faith'. When religious allegiance was a precondition for academic and other preferment, many were surely induced to profess loyalty to, for example, the Thirty-Nine Articles, when their true allegiances were quite otherwise. Nowadays there may well be much less hypocrisy; and when a philosopher, for example, professes a commitment to the current agenda of naturalism (the programme of explaining all phenomena without recourse to the supernatural), it seems very likely that inquiry into their private views would show them to be quite sincere atheists or agnostics.

The issue is not so much one of insincerity as of a certain kind of *compartmentalization*. People may, partly from habit, partly as a result of unspoken assumptions that underlie their daily discussions with friends and colleagues, be led almost imperceptibly to feel they are comfortable with the prevailing secular framework, and may be quite sincere in declaring it to be the basis of their worldview. But for all that, there may be certain deep structural features of the way they experience the world that, if fully reflected on, might turn out to be not so easy to fit into that secular framework.

This connects with the point raised in the previous section about our human responses to value. If we examine the phenomenology of ordinary experience among the vast majority of people of ordinary sensibilities (where these have not been blunted or distorted by deprivation or abuse or serious illness, or lack of proper nurturing in their early years), then I suggest that we will find a powerful and undeniable disposition to respond to the beauties of the natural world in (for want of a better term) a 'Wordsworthian' way: with joy and wonder and gratitude; and to respond to the demands of morality (to care for those in need, to respect justice, to avoid taking advantage of others) as imperatives which they cannot ignore or override, however much for selfish reasons, they might from time to time wish to. Reality, in short, presents itself to us, in the course of our own vivid human experience of the world, not as a meaningless concatenation of events, but as imbued with value and meaning – and, what is more, as a series of *demands*, which require a response from us in terms of how we live our lives. It may of course be possible to explain these things in a purely secular way (we shall look at this possibility in the following chapter). But however it is explained, the reality disclosed in the types of experience we are describing seems the very opposite of the 'disenchanted' world that is supposed to be the one we officially live in, according to the dominant secular culture. It is the very opposite of the random collection of rubble and debris that is supposed to have produced our world, along with us and our sensitivities, as an accidental by-product. It seems, instead, something remarkably close to the reality that is represented in the traditional theistic religions, a reality to which we respond with awe, as something wonderfully resonant with harmony and significance, and yet mysterious, elusive, bearing the stamp of the numinous.

So there is a kind of dissonance, I would suggest, between the 'official' secular naturalism which is the default position for self-respecting intellectuals in the Western world, and the character of the responses which, if we honestly interrogate ourselves, we find welling up within us. And it follows that although we may want to approach the question 'Why believe?' from a detached and neutral standpoint that soberly assesses the evidence for various religious doctrines, or the standard arguments for or against the existence of God, this programme for cold intellectual assessment arrives on the scene too late, as it were: we *already*, in a deep part of ourselves, either believe in something 'not ourselves that makes for righteousness',[21] or at least experience the world in many respects as if we did so believe. I propose, in the chapters that follow, to explore the resulting dissonance in more detail, and ask, as clearly as I can, how it can be resolved without loss of integrity on either side – in terms, on the one hand, of being true to the standards of

---

[21] Matthew Arnold, *Literature and Dogma* [1873].

critical inquiry and rational evaluation, and in terms, on the other hand, of being true to our deepest nature and the strength of our inner experience.

Chapter 2

Belief, Reason, Goodness

The alternation of day and night, the ceaseless round of celestial objects, the yearly cycle of the seasons, the falling leaves and the returning buds in spring, the inexhaustible power of all the different seeds, the beauty of the light, infinite varieties of colours, sounds, smells and tastes – anyone seeing and perceiving all this for the first time, could we but talk to him, would be stunned and overwhelmed with these miraculous wonders.

Augustine of Hippo[1]

1. Yearnings and their 'objective correlative'

I have so far argued that our human sensibilities, whether moral, aesthetic or religious, must at least be acknowledged as 'part of the picture', part of the reality we are trying to understand. But allowing this is one thing; conceding that such sensibilities have a genuine, existing *object* is another. The sceptic will say that whatever yearnings we may have for a reality that

---

[1] Augustine, *De utilitate credendi* ('On the Benefits of Believing') [AD 392], §34.

calls us towards beauty, truth and goodness, those yearnings are ultimately fruitless. The subjective feelings may be real enough (some product, or by-product, perhaps, of the way we happen to have evolved as biological creatures of a certain type); but what T. S. Eliot called the 'objective correlative' of such feelings simply does not exist.[2]

For the believer, things are very different. God, the God who is the object of worship in the Judaeo-Christian and Islamic traditions, is conceived of as the objective source of truth, beauty and goodness. He is, as the Epistle of James puts it, the giver of 'every good and every perfect gift'; in the words of the seventeenth-century Cambridge philosopher Peter Sterry, the stream of the divine love is the source of 'all truths, goodness, joys, beauties and blessedness'.[3] The idea of a unitary source of truth, beauty and goodness is an ancient one, going back to Plato, who urged us to struggle out of the dark 'cave' that is our normal human environment towards an eternal realm of value which he called the Forms, with a single Form of the Good at its apex. Aristotle, though rejecting the theory of the Forms, says much that is reminiscent of Plato's unifying approach; for example, he insists on the unity of the virtues – a doctrine which suggests that many seemingly disparate kinds

---

[2] 'Objective correlative' was a term introduced by T. S. Eliot in his essay 'Hamlet and His Problems' [1919] and defined as the set of objects that will set off a specific emotion in the reader.

[3] Epistle General of James [*c.* AD 50], 1:17: 'Every good and every perfect gift is from above, coming down from the father of lights.' Peter Sterry, *A Discourse of the Freedom of the Will* [1675]; repr. in Taliaferro and Teply (eds), *Cambridge Platonist Spirituality*, p. 179.

of goodness are at some deeper level interconnected. Moving down to the Middle Ages, Thomas Aquinas asserts that being and goodness are inter-convertible: *omne ens qua ens est bonum* ('every being *qua* being is good'). And in the early-modern period René Descartes, again following Plato (through the medium of St Augustine), makes the closest possible link between the good and the true: the nature of truth and of goodness is such that, once we clearly perceive them, they both constrain our judgement (to assent to the true, to desire the good): in both cases, says Descartes, a great light in the intellect generates a great propensity in the will.[4]

But is all this simply ancient history? Today, many people would probably regard the idea that goodness, truth and beauty are interconnected as outlandish. They might allow it a sentimental value, and might quote with a sort of wistful nostalgia the poet Keats's famous lines,

> Beauty is truth, truth beauty, that is all
> Ye know on Earth or ever need to know;[5]

but they would be unlikely to allow it a serious place in their belief system. The fact remains, however, that there are certain remarkable properties that truth, beauty and goodness all share. In the first place, they are all what philosophers call

---

4 Plato, *Republic* [375 BC], Bk V; Aristotle, *Nicomachean Ethics* [325 BC], Bk VI, Ch. 13; Aquinas, *Summa theologiae* [1266–73], Ia, 5, 3; René Descartes, *Meditations* [1641], Fourth Meditation.

5 John Keats, 'Ode on a Grecian Urn' [1819].

normative notions – they carry with them the sense of a *require-ment* or a *demand*. Some languages, Latin for example, have a special grammatical form, called the gerundive, to express this notion. Thus, *amandus* (from *amare*, to love) means not just that something is loved, or even that it is 'lovable' (in the rather weak sense that it tends to be loved or is apt to be loved), but rather that it is *to be loved*, that it ought to be loved. This kind of 'gerundive' flavour seems to attach to truth: the true is that which is worthy of belief – *to be believed*. And similarly the beau-tiful is that which is worthy of admiration, *to be admired*, and the good is that which is worthy of choice, *to be pursued*. Truth, beauty and goodness therefore seem to be rather 'queer' proper-ties (as the late Oxford philosopher John Mackie once put it[6]): they have this odd, magnetic aspect – they somehow have 'to-be-pursuedness' built into them. Why is this odd? Because it seems incompatible with any purely *naturalistic* or scientific account of these properties: for it is not easy to see how a purely natural or empirically definable item could have this strange 'normativity' or choice-worthiness somehow packed into it. So it starts to look as if thinking about these normative concepts is sooner or later going to take us beyond the purely natural or empirical domain.

In addition to their having this 'gerundive' or 'normative' force, truth, beauty and goodness appear to be *objective* prop-erties – they seem to hold independently of what you or I or anyone else may happen to think or to want or to prefer. They seem to presuppose an objective order of value that is logically

---

[6] J. Mackie, *Ethics: Inventing Right and Wrong*, Ch 1, §9.

independent of the beliefs and desires human beings may happen to have at any given time. Now with regard to such objectivism, there has been a remarkable shift in the philosophical climate over the past half-century or so. In the decades following the Second World War, when philosophy was slowly emerging from the shadow of logical positivism, moral beliefs ('value judgements', as people often pejoratively called them) were often dismissed as subjective – either mere expressions of emotion, mere grunts of approval or disapproval, or no more than 'pseudo-properties', masking our own personal desires and preferences. Later on, with the rise of postmodernism, even truth became suspect, and was downgraded to no more than a honorific label that a given culture chooses to bestow on its favoured assertions. But it is very striking how the popularity of these subjectivist creeds has faded in more recent times. Relativistic views of truth turned out to be self-defeating; while in ethics, subjectivism ran into a host of logical difficulties and is now on the wane, eclipsed by a growing number of neo-objectivist theories. To everyone's surprise, the growing consensus among philosophers is that some kind of objectivism of truth and of value is correct.

To be sure, objectivism does not in itself take us to a religious or theistic account of the source of that objectivity. There are many contemporary philosophers who reject theism but nevertheless want to claim that objective values somehow exist independently in their own right. Thus, one recent ethical theorist tells us that values are 'a brute fact about the way the world works'; another asserts that they are 'part of the furniture of the universe'.[7] Yet while this kind of moral realism is perhaps a theoretical possibility, unless the bald claim that values 'just exist' can be convincingly fleshed out, it seems to make the relationship between values and the rest of the 'furniture' of the universe very obscure.[8] To put it very crudely, are we supposed to think that values somehow float around, alongside planets and stars and galaxies? It is one thing to say they exist, but *how* do they exist, and what is their relationship to other things? A possible answer, suggested by some philosophers, is that we should think of them as purely abstract objects, perhaps rather like triangles or prime numbers. So if we are prepared to accept that abstract mathematical entities exist (waiting to be discovered and investigated by mathematicians), could we not perhaps accept that abstract values exist (waiting to be investigated by moralists)? Yet this kind of approach seems to invoke one mysterious fact (the existence of objective mathematical realities) in order to explain another (the existence of moral realities).[9]

---

[7] See R. Shafer-Landau, *Moral Realism* [2003]: moral standards 'just are correct'; they are 'a brute fact about the way the world works' (pp. 46, 48). For the 'part of the furniture' view, see E. J. Wielenberg, *Value and Virtue in a Godless Universe* [2005], p. 52.

[8] In fairness, Shafer-Landau is candid enough to acknowledge that bald, 'brute fact' ethical realism is a theory with 'very limited explanatory resources' (p. 48).

[9] The idea of the genuine 'reality' of abstract objects has a long philosophical history, going back to Plato (see *Republic*, Book V), but that does not make it any more intuitively plausible. Compare John McDowell's strictures against the kind of 'rampant Platonism' that posits a sui-generis world of values and reasons somehow existing independently of the natural world we inhabit (*Mind and World* [1995], p. 83).

What is more, to return to the idea of 'normative' or 'gerundive' force, it is surely remarkable that parts of reality should, as it were, have authority over us, which *has to be acknowledged whether we like it or not*. This certainly seems to apply to the necessary truths of logic and mathematics. However much we might want to escape them, we can avoid them only at the cost of talking nonsense or committing fallacies; for they are, as the nineteenth-century logician Gottlob Frege put it, 'boundary stones that our thought can overflow, but not dislodge'.[10] And somewhat similarly (at least in this one respect), moral truths seem to command our allegiance whether we like it or not. We can no doubt start to engage in cruel behaviour, and even develop a taste for it, but that does not show that cruelty has ceased to be wrong, but only that we have become corrupt. The wrongness of cruelty is inescapable, and cannot be dislodged by any human act or desire. Such facts are part of the reason why the truths of mathematics and of morality were traditionally called 'eternal verities': their timeless, necessary, objective and authoritative (or 'normative') status is beyond our reach to tamper with. Hence the initial appeal of the traditional metaphysical picture that regards them as stemming from an eternal and necessary being – God. Such a picture, whatever its other problems, at least seems more ontologically satisfying than the positing of goodness as a kind of abstract property that somehow exists independently of any substance. (Very crudely, an ontology where properties inhere in substances, whether divine or mundane, seems intuitively more satisfying than one

---

10 G. Frege, *The Basic Laws of Arithmetic* [1893], p. 13.

where they just float around without anything to belong to.)

But perhaps a theistic grounding for objective value can be resisted by another route, which has enjoyed growing popularity among moral philosophers in the last ten years or so. This has become known as a 'buck-passing' account of value, because it shifts the focus away from terms like 'good' and 'ought' to much less puzzling and more down-to-earth notions that seem to underpin them. What makes a knife good is simply that it has certain ordinary natural or observable features (such as sharpness) which give me reason to choose it, if I want to cut something.[11] And similarly, what makes charity good, for example, is simply that the relevant actions have certain ordinary natural properties (e.g. reducing suffering) that give me reason to perform them.

Yet although goodness and badness are obviously connected with ordinary features of actions in this way (the ordinary observable features providing *reasons* for us to choose or avoid things), it is unfortunately all too clear that many people are not responsive to such reasons. Many people delight in cruel or vicious behaviour; and the suffering of others that *we* may regard as a reason for them to desist, simply is not recognized by them as a reason to stop. We may reply: 'Yes, but whatever they say or feel, the suffering *is* a reason, a conclusive reason, for them to desist'; but then we seem to be appealing to some kind of moral demand that remains in force no matter what – no matter how many people transgress it, or refuse to recognize it. In short, although the 'buck-passing' account of value seems

---

[11] T. Scanlon, *What we Owe to Each Other* [1998], pp. 95ff. Cf. P. J. Stratton-Lake, *Ethical Intuitionism* [2002], p. 15f.

right in grasping how goodness and badness point beyond themselves to ordinary features of actions that provide reasons to choose or avoid them, it does not appear to explain how some of those reasons possess *conclusive normative power*.

2. From benefits to reasons

Questions about the structure of moral properties, and the basis of their objectivity and normativity, are notoriously tricky ones, and they may seem to have landed us in philosophically daunting and difficult territory; but the main trajectory of our argument so far has in fact been relatively straightforward. It may be helpful to retrace our steps. We began in Chapter 1 by reflecting on the widespread feeling that religious allegiance offers certain benefits to the believer, in the form of encouragement and comfort. At first sight this seemed irrelevant to the question, 'Why believe?', since, whatever benefits it might promise, belief is not something that can be adopted 'just like that'. But it then emerged that there might, as Pascal suggested, be strategies for turning oneself into a believer. An objection was then raised against pursuing this line, namely that the question 'Why believe?' surely ought to be tackled by reference not to benefits, but to reasons and evidence. The next stage in the argument was to suggest that the deep and widespread yearning of the human spirit for truth, beauty and goodness cannot be dismissed as irrelevant to the question of evidence, since such a yearning seems to be part of our human nature, and is hence one of the phenomena that any rational belief-system must accommodate in one way or another. This in turn led us on to ask whether the yearning in question could be explained away as an aberration – a yearning without an object – or whether it points us towards something like a traditional theistic conception of an eternal source of truth, beauty and goodness, a source towards which we are drawn as the goal of our yearning. The last step was simply to note the current philosophical groundswell in favour of a return to moral objectivism, and to suggest that traditional theism may offer a more secure metaphysical underpinning for such objectivism than the alternatives currently on offer. So, starting from considering the benefits of religious belief, we have been led by incremental steps towards reflecting on certain fundamental human needs and yearnings; and thinking about the object of those yearnings has led us at least a little way towards possible rational *reasons* for belief in God.

3. God as source

At this point, many critics will want to question whether the idea of a theistic 'underpinning' for value is coherent or intelligible. What exactly can it mean to say that God is the *source* of truth, beauty and goodness? Well, the most important thing it implies, to begin with, is a firm denial of relativism. If an eternal, necessary being, existing independently of us, is the source of truth, then this rules out pragmatic and relativistic conceptions according to which truth is simply what works for us, or what is currently accepted in our culture circle. And similarly, beauty, if stemming from God, cannot simply be 'in the eye of the beholder' – just a function of the subjective tastes of various human beings. And similarly, goodness, and value generally, cannot be dependent merely on our personal or societal preferences, let alone something we can create by our own dynamic acts of will, as Friedrich Nietzsche maintained.[12] All these things – truth, beauty and goodness – must be, on the contrary, objectively based.

So far, perhaps, so good. Believing in God is *consistent* with a belief in the objectivity of goodness and other values, and this (if objectivism about values is correct) provides at least some sort of reason (albeit a rather weak one) for theistic belief. Building on that, we might move to a much stronger and more telling reason for believing in God if we could go on to show that invoking God provides a satisfying *explanation,* or even the *best available explanation,* for the objectivity and normativity of goodness and other values.

Unfortunately for theism, however, it is not immediately clear how it can lay claim to an explanation of this kind. For *how* exactly, one might ask, is God supposed to function as the 'source' of truth, beauty and goodness? God should not, surely, be thought of as 'creating' these things by some arbitrary act of will or preference – that would begin to look like a sort of Nietzschean subjectivism transposed to the celestial realm. Instead, to start with the case of truth, the theist must presumably envisage God as the source of truth in so far as he establishes those objective features of reality in virtue of which the propositions that rational beings assert can be true or false. God, in other words, does not 'create truth', whatever that

---

12 Friedrich Nietzsche, *Beyond Good and Evil* [1886], §203.

would mean, but creates the *truth-makers*, as it were. He creates (as the first verse of Genesis has it) the 'heavens and the earth', the whole vast evolving process of the cosmos;[13] and in consequence of the resulting properties and configurations of stars, planets, plants, molecules, atoms and so on, certain beliefs or propositions now have the property of being true or false. That seems (relatively, at least) quite straightforward.[14]

What about beauty? Perhaps the simplest picture would be to think of God creating beauty analogously to the way in which a human creative artist is responsible for it – namely by creating beautiful objects. When an artist paints a beautiful picture, he does so by endowing it with beauty-making properties – harmony of colour, symmetry, rhythm, proportionality, and so on. Again, it is not beauty itself that is created, whatever that would mean, but rather those objects or entities with their relevant properties and qualities in virtue of which they are beautiful. The Andromeda galaxy, seen though a telescope, is extraordinarily beautiful – a coruscating spiral of millions of blazing stars of different hues, wheeling around in an infinitely complex gravitational dance. The Psalmist could not of course see this, but he could see (as many of us sadly now no longer can owing to pollution) something of the awesome splendour of what we now call our 'local' galaxy:

---

[13] The creation story in Genesis is not in competition with evolutionary theory; there is long theological tradition, going back at least to St Augustine, according to which the 'six days' of creation do not need to be construed literally (Augustine, *De Genesi ad litteram* [401–14], Bk IV).

[14] A more complex account will be required of the kind of truth enjoyed by the eternal and necessary truths of logic and mathematics, and theists differ among themselves about what exactly is God's relation to them.

'the heavens declare the glory of the Lord, and the firmament shows his handiwork.'[15]

So beauty, like truth, is comparatively easy for the believer to see as divinely sourced, in the sense just explicated. But what about goodness, and in particular moral goodness? Following the model so far adopted, the theist will want to say that God creates goodness by performing actions with good-making properties – for example, he 'protects strangers and supports the fatherless and the widow' (Psalm 146 [145]:9). He is the source of goodness in this sense; and in addition, of course, he brings into existence creatures like us who themselves have the power to perform such actions. They may not always do so, because they are free to refrain (or even to do things with bad-making properties). But when they do what is good, they are fulfilling one of the purposes for which God created them. In this sense, then, God may be said to be the source of the goodness not just of his own acts but of that which pertains to the acts of his creatures. (This raises the question, which will be left aside for the present, of why God is not also the source of the evil acts performed by humans; there are many responses to this which are familiar from the theodicy literature, most hinging on the idea that God does not create anyone with the intention that they should perform such actions, albeit foreseeing that they may do so.)

Now if we adopt the above picture, we seem to be implicitly adopting the kind of 'buck-passing' account of goodness referred to earlier. As we saw, the focus in such accounts is not on

---

15 Psalm 19 [18]:1.

goodness itself, but on the various good-making properties in virtue of which something counts as good. So, to revert to our non-moral example, to say that a knife is good is not to refer to some special property it has in addition to its ordinary empirically observable properties; rather 'the buck is passed', and the goodness devolves down to the ordinary properties (sharpness, strength, durability) that make it fit to be chosen as a cutting implement. In creating a knife with these properties, a human craftsman has *automatically* thereby made a good knife. So similarly with moral goodness, the believer will want to say that God, by enacting merciful or beneficent actions, or by creating humans who can perform merciful or beneficent actions, automatically qualifies as a source of goodness in the world. Nothing more, as it were, is needed. This is consistent with the first chapter of Genesis, where it is said of God, looking on his creation, that he 'saw that it was good' – *not* that he decreed or ordained that it should qualify as good. God does not have to enact any additional decrees in order to create goodness; rather he creates the world as it is, with all its various good-making properties, and then (so to speak) he can just *see*, in virtue of those created properties, that it is good.

But now the following question arises. If the goodness devolves down to the various observable good-making properties in this way, then don't we have to say that it exists in the world *whether or not that world was created by God*? And does not that cast serious doubt about the idea of God as *the* source of goodness? For as we look around us (the atheist may urge), there in front of us are the good-making properties, existing already in the ordinary empirical features of the world: flints are sharp, and therefore apt for cutting; people sometimes choose to perform actions which help other people. These relevant good-making features indisputably exist, whether the world was created by God, or whether instead it arose by chance or some other impersonal mechanism. So (it might be argued) doesn't that make God, in a certain sense, redundant? It seems, in other words, as if we don't need God as the putative 'source' of goodness; we just need the relevant purely natural features in virtue of which things count as good, and that is that.[16]

I think there is something right about this move, but something that it leaves out. It is right that our pursuit of goodness is not a matter of seeking some mysterious extra quality in addition to the observable features of actions and objects, but rather involves a careful investigation and assessment of their relevant good-making properties. So the atheist and the theist are, as it were, on equal footing when it comes to assessing what objects and actions are good or bad: the available tools are not some hotline to a special divinely sourced property of goodness, but ordinary human observation of the natural world, and ordinary human reasoning about the features of this world and the actions of the people within it. Ethics is a matter of human inquiry, just like science. It is a subject of rational

---

16 One of the most prominent of theistic philosophers, Richard Swinburne, though regarding God as *a* source of moral obligation (since 'his command to us to do some action makes it obligatory to do that action when it would not otherwise be obligatory'), considers that God is not *the* (sole) source of goodness or of obligation, since 'many truths of morality hold whether or not there is a God'. He cites the cases of feeding the starving and keeping promises: the first is clearly good, the second clearly obligatory, and these truths hold 'independently of God'. *Was Jesus God?* [2008], p. 11.

debate, in which proper reasons for and against certain courses of action need to be marshalled using our ordinary human capacities, and our ordinary human perception of the various natural features of objects and actions which make them good or bad. So much, I think, is entirely correct (and, incidentally, it happens to be a welcome result, since it seems conducive to constructive debate that theists and atheists should see themselves as being on 'equal footing' in this way when it comes to deciding moral issues).

Despite this, there will nevertheless be something questionable for the theist about the implication that God is, as it were, redundant when it comes to questions about goodness, or that God has no special role to play as the source of goodness. To begin with, the theist will of course want to say that even if the buck-passing account of ordinary natural good-making features is correct, God still retains an all-pervasive general role, since his action was still required to create the world with all its natural features in the first place. God still performs the mysterious metaphysical act which (as Herbert McCabe puts it) makes the difference between its existence and non-existence.[17]

But with that important proviso in place, should the theist go on to concede that once the world is in existence, the goodness or badness of things can be 'read off', as it were, from its ordinary natural features, without any need for reference to God as its source (except in so far as he is regarded as the source of the universe existing at all)? In some ways this is a tempting option. It would mean that the theist and the atheist

---

[17] Herbert McCabe, *Faith within Reason* [2006], pp. 74–6.

will see themselves as inhabiting exactly the same cosmos, a cosmos which naturally possesses some good-making and some bad-making features; but that the theist merely (!) adds the extra metaphysical claim that the world was divinely created.[18] Possibly this is as far as the theist should go. But, without being wholly sure about it, I am inclined to think (as I suggested a moment ago) that, tempting as it may be, this view leaves something out. What I think it leaves out is any explanation of *why* certain features of actions or agents should be good-making features, not merely in the weak sense that they provide conditional reasons for choosing such actions, but in the stronger sense that they provide a *conclusive* or *unconditional* reason for choice,[19] one that requires our compliance.

For in a random or impersonal universe, why should the fact that an action oppresses the weak and helpless be a reason – a conclusive reason – against performing it? Or why should the fact that an act is one of forgiveness towards someone who is sincerely sorry for having injured us be a reason, a conclusive

---

[18] Compare McCabe: 'So far as the kind of world we have is concerned, the atheist and the theist will expect to see exactly the same features'. *Faith within Reason,* p. 76.

[19] Compare Immanuel Kant's famous distinction between various types of imperative in his *Groundwork* [1785], Ch. 2, nicely summarized in H. J. Paton's edition as follows: 'some objective principles are *conditioned* by a will for some end; that is to say, they would necessarily be willed by an agent *if* he willed that end . . . Some are *unconditioned* . . . and have the form "I ought to do such and such" without any *if* as a prior condition' (p. 27). Kant called the first type of imperative 'hypothetical', the second 'categorical', but the term 'categorical imperative' is now so overlaid with complications arising from Kantian scholarship that I prefer to avoid it for present purposes.

reason, for performing it? How can such descriptive features of things have this compelling, action-guiding force, this specially strong version of the magnetic quality that we noted earlier, this categorical, built-in 'to-be-doneness'. For many atheists (taking their cue from John Mackie) the 'queerness' of such supposed conclusive reason-giving force will be taken as a reason for concluding that genuine objective moral properties do not really exist – that they are in the end specious, a mere projection of our own preferences.[20] That is a radical position, which faces many philosophical problems, but at least it has the courage of its convictions. But for those who do not want to take this radical subjectivist route, for the increasing number of moral philosophers of an atheist stripe who are drawn to objectivism in ethics, some account is surely required of *how* some natural observable features of things are endowed not just with provisional or instrumental but with unconditional or categorical action-guiding force. How is it that the fact that something involves the deliberate infliction of distress provides a conclusive reason not to do it, and one that applies whatever aims or projects I happen to have chosen? How is it that the property of helping the weak and afflicted provides (assuming there are no prior claims on my resources) a conclusive reason

---

20 Mackie, *Ethics*, Ch. 1. Interestingly, Mackie conceded that if there *were* genuine moral properties, and an authentic link between something's having a certain empirical property and its being objectively right or wrong, then this would be an argument for the existence of God as their source: Mackie, *The Miracle of Theism* [1982], p. 118. (There are of course differences between 'good/bad' and 'right/wrong', but important though these are, they will be ignored for present purposes, since they do not affect the general structure of the argument we are considering.)

to perform a given action? What establishes this weird or 'queer' connection between an observable feature of the natural world and this kind of strong normative power to require us to act?

For the theist, there is an answer. If God himself is in his essential nature merciful, compassionate, just and loving, then when we humans act in the ways just mentioned we are drawn closer to God, the source of our being, and the source of all that is good. Such acts command our allegiance in the strongest way, since they bring us nearer to the 'home' where our true peace and fulfilment lie; and, conversely, in setting our face against them, we are cutting ourselves off from our true destiny, from the ultimate basis of joy and meaningfulness in our lives. If, on the other hand, there is no God, if God is 'dead', then there might (as Nietzsche frighteningly suggested) be conclusive reasons to steel ourselves *against* impulses of love and mercy, to harden our hearts against compassion and forgiveness, since such sentiments might get in the way of our will to power, or our passion for self-realization, or some other grand project we happen to have.[21] Only if those features we call good-making point us towards the true goal of our existence will we be able to make sense of their having, in addition to their observable aspects, a normative force which commands our allegiance whether we like it or not, independently of our own contingent inclinations. Only if the universe has a moral teleology behind it will moral goodness or righteousness really exist – as something we have conclusive reason to choose –

21 See, for example, Nietzsche, *Beyond Good and Evil* [1886], §37.

rather than merely dissolving away into features that are suitable for furthering whatever projects we may happen to have adopted, or whatever purposes we may happen to have set ourselves.

4. The best explanation?

Even if it is conceded that a theistic metaphysics provides *a* viable framework for understanding value, many will ask why we should suppose it is the only viable framework, or the best one. It would take a volume in its own right to examine and compare all the sophisticated competitor theories of value currently in the field. But at least some general points can, I think, be made. Crudely naturalistic accounts (which simply equate moral properties with empirical properties) seem unlikely to work, for the reasons already discussed, since they do not have the resources to explain how purely empirical features of reality can have authoritative or normative force. But the kind of more sophisticated buck-passing account mentioned earlier does seem in a stronger position: the natural observable properties of things are seen as having the 'second-order' property of providing reasons for action in virtue of their ordinary natural features.

As already indicated, I think such buck-passing accounts are true, but incomplete. They do not tell us, in the moral arena, *why* certain features of actions provide conclusive reasons for choosing to do them. Ultimately, in a godless universe what I have reason to do will depend merely on the set of contingent desires I happen to have developed, and the set of inclinations and preferences I and my society happen to have evolved to have. Ethics, in short, will be subject to what Bernard Williams called a '*radical contingency*'.[22]

Yet is this really so troubling? Some recent philosophers who are drawn to objectivism in ethics have pointed out that, notwithstanding the contingencies of personal and social development, the reasons for action still remain objective and external, not personal or subjective. For example, what gives me reason to thank you for doing me a good turn does not hinge on what contingent beliefs or desires I have, but instead is a perfectly objective or external matter: the plain external fact that you did me a service. This may be true, but one still wants to ask: how do such so-called objective or 'external' reasons get their normative force? The moral philosopher John Skorupski has recently given the example of a character, Tom, who has been helped by Mary, but who simply has no sense of gratitude – he simply doesn't 'get' what it is all about. Do we want to say that Tom has reason to thank Mary? Skorupski argues that our response to this question is 'interestingly uncertain'. On the one hand we want to say 'Of course he does – look what she has done for him!' But on the other hand, we can understand the basis for answering 'No' – namely that Tom just doesn't see the reason-giving force of the fact that she has done him a good turn. So Skorupski concludes that 'only considerations which

---

22 Bernard Williams, *Truth and Truthfulness* [2002], p. 20.

the agent has the ability to recognize, for him or herself, "from within", *as* reasons, can *be* reasons for that agent".[23]

If we accept this, it seems to bring us back to the 'radical contingency of the ethical'. What count as reasons for us to behave in certain ways will depend on the way we see things, which in turn depends on the way our individual and social development happens to have gone. And the possibility that people and societies might have developed different evaluative outlooks undermines the thought that certain features of actions *must* always provide conclusive moral reasons to choose or avoid them. So (on the secularist view we are considering) there is ultimately no room in ethics for the idea that, in our attempts to pursue the good, we have got something objectively right – in the way that we believe we can get things right (or at least make progress towards getting things right) in science.[24] Morality will have no stable foundation, only a fluctuating and shifting pattern of individual and social preferences and dispositions.

From a theistic perspective, this alarming contingency of the ethical, the threat to objectivity, and the worrying gap between the kind of knowledge we can have in science and in ethics, are all avoided. In science, as Descartes and other theistic rationalists maintained, we can gain a basic insight, through the mathematical awareness innately implanted in us, of the rational patterns which govern the physical universe; and similarly in ethics, in the light of the fundamental moral awareness

[23] John Skorupski, 'Internal Reasons and the Scope of Blame', in A. Thomas (ed.), *Bernard Williams*, pp. 73–103, at p. 88.

[24] See Bernard Williams, *Ethics and the Limits of Philosophy* [1985], Ch. 8; see further Adrian Moore, in Thomas (ed.), *Bernard Williams*, pp. 24–46.

implanted in us, we have the power to orient ourselves towards the good which lies at the heart of reality. The strongest kind of objectivity of ethics is secured, just as it is in science (though this need not of course mean that ethical questions have quick and easy answers, any more than is the case with scientific questions).

A further reason why a theistic metaphysics is fundamentally hospitable to the idea of genuine objectively normative standards like rationality and goodness (hospitable in a way I believe secular world views are unlikely to be) is that ultimate reality, on the theistic view, is *personal* and *purposive*, rather than blind, irrational, neutral, random or blank – which is in the end what an alternative atheistical worldview must take it to be. Thus, the two features of God that are prominent above all others in the Christian Gospels (especially in the fourth and most metaphysical of the Gospels) are reason (*logos*) and love (*agape*). These are features that are very closely connected with attributes (intelligence, loving concern) that are irreducibly personal; and indeed, in the Christian picture, they are supremely manifested in the human world in a particular person, the person of Christ.

Humans are (on any showing) an imperfect species, who are clearly not always disposed to conform their lives to reason and to love; but if the cosmos ultimately reflects a divine teleology or goal-directedness, our lives, because of the way we were created, cannot flourish without them. That rationality and love are the sources behind the cosmos is not something that could be established by ordinary scientific inquiry (I shall say more about why this is so in the next chapter). Because of the 'transcendence' of God (the fact that the Creator is taken to be wholly 'other' than his creation), a long theological tradition maintains that we cannot fully grasp such properties as reason and love as they exist in the divine nature. And as for the Christian claim that their human face has been disclosed to us in a way we *can* grasp, in the person of Christ – this is a matter of revelation, and therefore of faith, rather than philosophical reason. The extraordinary claim of this cosmic intrusion of the divine into our human world is nonetheless made with unmistakable clarity in the fourth Gospel: the title of *to phôs tôn anthrôpôn* (the 'light of humankind'), identified with the *logos*, the eternal godhead in John 1:1–5, is directly appropriated by Christ, when he claims 'I am the light of the world' (*ego eimi to phôs tou kosmou*, John 8:12). In this context, the *ego eimi* ('I am') is the ancient signature of divinity, recapitulating God's self-disclosure to Moses as the source of the moral law.[25] Traditional theism has always insisted that there is an eternal source of goodness, truth and beauty behind the visible cosmos; and in its Christian form it insists that this source, though transcendent – dwelling in 'light inaccessible' (1 Timothy 6:16) – is made manifest in a human form, full of 'grace and truth', visible to human sight (John 1:14).

In a chapter that has been largely concerned with rather abstract philosophical questions about the nature and origins of goodness, we have plunged, right at the end, into the heart of a theological mystery, that of the Incarnation – the extraordinary idea that the eternal Word 'pitched its tent among us'

---

[25] In Exodus 3:14 (compare John 8:58).

(*eskênôsen en hêmin*; John 1:14). This flags up something distinctive about the nature of religious belief, which we shall need to come back to in our next chapter, namely the way in which it straddles the rational and the mystical domains: the believer has the boldness or (depending on your view) the incredible foolhardiness to pitch his tent on the boundary between the manifest and the ineffable. But this perhaps makes it appropriate to conclude the present phase of our discussion on a more cautious note. Because of the necessary gap between transcendent reality and any manifestation accessible to human understanding, the idea of a divine source of goodness (or indeed of truth and of beauty) is not, I think, something that can be fully explicated using the tools of philosophical reason alone. But if the argument of this chapter has been correct, it is at least consistent with what we can establish philosophically about moral goodness. And, crucially, it provides a *framework* that frees us from the threats of contingency and futility that lurk beneath the surface of supposedly self-sufficient and autonomous secular ethics. It offers us not a proof, but a hope that the 'cave' of our human world (to use Plato's image)[26] is not utterly sealed and closed, but that our flickering moral intimations reflect the ultimate source of all goodness (just as, on the theistic view, our logico-mathematical and our aesthetic intimations can, when suitably trained and purified, reflect the ultimate source of rationality and of beauty). The unqualified, unprovisional, non-contingent good-makingness of those ordinary natural features of our

---

[26] Plato, *Republic* [*c.* 380 BC], Bk VII.

human actions, in virtue of which they conform to the moral law, arises from this. By choosing such actions, and continuing to choose them, we conform to an intelligible, rational pattern, the pattern that a being of surpassing love and benevolence intended for us. Believing this may be partly a matter of faith, but it may also reflect a more coherent and compelling conception of the nature of goodness than anything else that is on offer.

Chapter 3

Belief and the Unknown

Just as the eyes of night-birds fail when the light of day appears, so it is with our soul's understanding of those things which are really clearest of all.

Aristotle[1]

1. The unknown God?

Si comprehendis, non est Deus, said Augustine: if you grasp him, he is not God.[2] An ancient tradition in theology has insisted that God cannot be encompassed by human thought. It is a tradition rooted in the Judaeo-Christian scriptures. God is the awesome, unnameable one, who told Moses 'no man may see me and live' (Exodus 33:20). He dwells, says St Paul, in 'light inaccessible': no man has seen him or can see him (1 Timothy 6:16). Philosophical reflection has tended to reinforce the theological and biblical idea that God must lie largely beyond our human reach: Aquinas famously argues that we can know the properties of God only by analogy; and the five ways or

---

[1] *Metaphysics* [*c.* 325 BC], Bk II, Ch. 1.
[2] Augustine, *Sermones* [392–430], 52, vi, 16 and 117, iii, 5.

proofs of God's existence which he offered have aptly been described as 'minimalist', since they do not specify the nature of God, but only an unknown, unobservable something which is the transcendent source of the various sequences we observe in the world. When God is invoked in this type of context it is in a way radically different from what happens when scientists offer causal explanations.[3] For René Descartes in the seventeenth century, following this Augustinian and Thomist lead, God is by his very nature not fully encompassable in our thought: he is like the mountain which our thought can reach, but not comprehend, just as we can touch a mountain but not put our arms round it.[4]

Perhaps not surprisingly, this idea of God as transcending our human ability to grasp him started to sound philosophical alarm bells in the eighteenth century, with the advent of the Enlightenment and its warnings about going beyond the proper limits of human inquiry. For Immanuel Kant, once we depart from the 'Island of Truth' (*Das Land der Wahrheit*) – the domain of empirical knowledge – and venture out into the stormy sea of metaphysical speculation, we are liable to be lost. The island of truth, says Kant,

> . . . is surrounded by a wide and stormy ocean, the native home of illusion, where many a fog bank and many a swiftly melting iceberg give the *deceptive appearance of farther shores*, deluding the adventurous seafarer ever

---

[3] Compare B. Davies, *Aquinas* [2002], p. 46, and A. Kenny, *What is Faith?* [1992], p. 111.

[4] Descartes, Letter to Mersenne of 27 May 1630.

anew with *empty hopes* and engaging him in enterprises which he can never abandon and yet is unable to carry to completion.[5]

Some decades earlier, David Hume had put a somewhat similar point, albeit in a rather more edged and ironic way, focusing directly on traditional theism:

> When we carry our speculations into the two eternities, before and after the present state of things: into the creation and formation of the universe, the existence and properties of spirits, the powers and operations of one universal Spirit existing without beginning and without end, omnipotent, omniscient, immutable, infinite, and incomprehensible – we must be far removed from the smallest tendency to scepticism not to be apprehensive that we have here got *quite beyond the reach of our faculties.*[6]

Among Hume's targets from his own immediate predecessors was the French philosopher and theologian Nicolas Malebranche, who in his *Recherche de la Vérité* (in a passage quoted by Hume) had stressed how far the deity must transcend any anthropomorphic conceptions. Just as we should not imagine God to be corporeal, Malebranche observed, so we should not

---

[5] Immanuel Kant, *Critique of Pure Reason* [1781/1787], A235/B294 (emphasis supplied).

[6] David Hume, *Dialogues Concerning Natural Religion* [*c*. 1755], Part I, §9; ed. Aiken, p. 9; emphasis supplied.

really describe him as a Mind or Spirit, since that invites comparison with a human mind. Rather, Malebranche suggested, we should think that 'just as He includes the perfections of matter without being material, so He includes the perfections of created spirits without being spirit – at least in the manner we conceive spirit'. So instead of trying to specify the nature of God via properties drawn from our human experience, which are bound to be misleading, we should content ourselves instead with saying he is pure Being, 'Being without restriction, Being infinite and universal.'[7]

Yet this notion of pure Being, or *ipsum esse*, though it goes back to Aquinas and has roots much earlier in Plato, is by no means obviously a coherent one. Arguably it boils down to an incomplete or defective formula, the mere introduction of what logicians call an existential quantifier ('There is an x such that ...'), but with nothing to complete the proposition. Hume expresses his doubts by saying that the question 'can never be concerning the *being* of the Deity, but only his *nature*'.[8] In other words, we need to be able to say at least *something* about the nature of this supposedly existing *je ne sais quoi*. And yet here is the problem. The long theistic tradition drawn on by Malebranche insists that our human framework of predication is inadequate to express the nature of the deity – and yet the human framework is all we have; and it is a framework, moreover, which is, necessarily, shaped by our human experience. As Hume puts it, anticipating Kant, in what might be a slogan for

---

7 Nicolas Malebranche, *Recherche de la Vérité* [1674], Bk 3, Ch. 9.
8 Hume, *Dialogues*, Part II, §3.

the Enlightenment: 'Our ideas reach no farther than our experience.'[9]

Yet why exactly should it be so problematic to suppose that the deity transcends our human experience? After all, are there not many parts of reality (electrons or neutrinos, for example) that elude our capacity to experience them, at any rate directly? We know, for example, that concepts drawn from human experience, such as 'wave' and 'particle', are not really applicable to such micro-entities, except by analogy; so why should not God be such an entity – not to be directly experienced, but hypothesized as the hidden cause for what we do experience?

Unfortunately for the theist, these scientific parallels do not quite work. For although we have no direct empirical contact with the world of micro-particles, we are able to observe and detect all sorts of directly measurable effects of those entities, describe them in precise mathematical and quantitative terms, and make experiential predictions of astonishing accuracy about what will be experienced as a result of their presence or absence. Granted, Hume's view that 'our ideas reach no farther than our experience' may need some qualification, if it is taken to mean 'no further than our *direct* experience'; but the scientist who accepts the general spirit of Hume, if not the letter, can nevertheless claim to have some idea of these entities based on *indirect* experience. We may not *fully* comprehend the nature of physical micro-entities, but there is a reasonable case for saying we at least partly comprehend them: they are not unknown transcendent entities, but are

---

9 Hume, *Dialogues*, Part II, §4.

immanent in the world, components which constitute the ordinary natural macro-objects of our daily experience.

Nevertheless, once we concede that there are entities accepted even by the hard-nosed scientist which we do not wholly comprehend, and whose nature cannot be fully reduced to what we experience, then the theist may hope to get a foot back in the door. If there are real and genuine entities that *partially* transcend our human ability to comprehend them, then why should we rule out entities, like the divine nature, which *wholly* transcend our human grasp? What precisely is so wrong about invoking what Hume (again with his characteristic irony) called, 'the adorably mysterious and incomprehensible nature of the Supreme Being'?[10]

The stage is now set for what we may term Hume's killer argument – an argument that threatens at a stroke to undermine the entire 'apophatic' strategy that stretches from Augustine down to Malebranche (apophatic theology asserts the breakdown of all human speech in the face of the unknowability of God).[11] The killer argument appears in the mouth of Cleanthes at the start of Part IV of the *Dialogues Concerning Natural Religion*. It seems strange, says Cleanthes, that supporters of religion should insist on the mysterious nature of God; for 'How do you mystics, who maintain the absolute incomprehensibility of the Deity, differ from sceptics or atheists, who assert that the first cause of all is unknown and unintelligible?'[12] So far from

---

10 Hume, *Dialogues*, Part II, §5.
11 Compare Denys Turner, *The Darkness of God* [1995], p. 19.
12 Hume, *Dialogues*, Part IV, §1.

being in a position to defend the cause of religion against its critics, such mystics 'are, in a word, *atheists without knowing it*.'[13] To believe in an unknown and unknowable God is extensionally equivalent to believing in no God at all.

2. Hume's critique

Devastating as Hume's killer argument seems to be on first deployment, its precise force is not, on reflection, entirely clear. There are, I think, two possible interpretations of it. On the first, he is deriving it from a radical empiricist thesis about the limits of meaning; on the second, he is deriving it from a radical empiricist view of the limits of knowledge. Let us briefly look at each reading in turn.

The first, semantic, reading sees Hume as a kind of proto-positivist, insisting that our ideas can only be meaningful if they are drawn from experience. If, as per the Humean slogan quoted earlier, 'our ideas reach no further than our experience', then any idea which wholly transcends the world of experience must presumably lack any genuine cognitive content. This would explain Hume's famous peroration at the end of Section XII of the *Treatise*. The closed, *a priori* reasonings of mathematics, on the one hand, and inferences from actual observation on the other, exhaust the proper sphere of human inquiry. Any metaphysical speculation which tries to go beyond these

---

13 Hume, *Dialogues*, Part IV, §3.

boundaries should be committed 'to the flames: for it can contain nothing but sophistry and illusion'.[14]

Yet interpreting all this as an early form of verificationism about meaning faces considerable difficulties. In the first place, if Hume is read this way, he runs into the obvious problem the logical positivists were later to face in the twentieth century: if the observable or the empirically verifiable defines the limits of meaning, how can Hume's own (supposed) assertion of his radical empiricism about meaning itself be meaningful? But quite apart from this, there is a textual problem, namely that the wording of our killer argument from the *Dialogues* does not sound very appropriate, if the challenge is supposed to be that the mystic is talking nonsense; for Hume's actual question, as phrased, is not whether the mystical position can be made to make sense, but how the position can avoid collapsing into *atheism or scepticism*. The introduction of the latter term is, I think, highly significant from the point of view of interpreting Hume's stance. For the *sceptic* about a given claim is not someone who dismisses it as meaningless (in which case there would be nothing to be sceptical *about*), but rather one who merely thinks we cannot *know* whether or not it is true.

This brings us to the second, epistemological, reading of Hume. As a general line of Humean interpretation, this achieved prominence some years ago, with the publication of John Wright's *The Sceptical Realism of David Hume*.[15] In brief,

---

[14] David Hume, *An Enquiry Concerning Human Understanding* [1748], Section XII, part 3.

[15] J. Wright, *The Sceptical Realism of David Hume* [1983]. Cf. Galen Strawson, *The Secret Connexion: Causation, Realism and David Hume* [1989].

what Wright argued was that, with respect to causation, for example, Hume is not denying the intelligibility or the possibility of secret underlying connexions in nature, but is making the epistemic point that, since our knowledge is necessarily based on observation and experience, if such connexions existed *we could never know anything about them*. This makes much better sense than the 'verificationist' reading of many of the things that Hume says about the limits of science, which seem entirely focused on questions of knowledge, not of semantics. Thus, he says in a famous passage in the *Treatise* that though the scientist may aim to reduce all observed phenomena to a set of simple laws or principles, any attempt to speculate further about the ultimate reality responsible for these general truths is in vain: the most perfect natural science only 'staves off our ignorance', since 'the ultimate springs and principles' of reality are 'totally shut up from human curiosity and enquiry'.[16]

If this 'sceptical realist' interpretation is right, then Hume's complaint against the mystic is that the result of his placing of God in an entirely transcendent and ineffable domain, beyond the scope of any predicates drawn from human observation, is that such a being, if it exists, is one of whom we can have no possible knowledge. It is, in short, an argument for *agnosticism*, *not* for outright atheism. Atheism, I take it, is either an assertion that theism is incoherent, or an assertion that theism is false; whereas the agnostic allows that there may exist a God,

---

16 David Hume, *A Treatise of Human Nature* [1739–40], Book I, Part iv, Section 3, Para. 7.

but insists we can't know anything about his possible existence or nature. Hume would be conceding that there may be a God, just as there may be some other 'ultimate springs and principles of nature', but pointing out that our experience is, and must remain, 'entirely silent' about such things.

The so-called killer argument, in short, turns out (on this view) to be far less disturbing than it at first seemed to be for the theist – less of a fatal blow and more of a shrugging of the shoulders. Admittedly, if Hume is right, God turns out to be beyond the reach of human knowledge; but that is also true, for Hume, of a great many other things people are inclined to believe – for example that 'the perceptions of the senses are produced by external objects' (e.g. my impression of a chair is produced by a real chair). On this, and 'all matters of a like nature', Hume observes, 'experience is and must be entirely silent'.[17] If this is what the Enlightenment critique of religion amounts to, then it is one that many believers might be happy to live with, since it puts God beyond the realm of empirical science, but not beyond the realm of faith. Indeed, once the sting of Hume's killer argument has been drawn, it becomes quite compatible with the position taken by Immanuel Kant, who famously remarked namely that he found it necessary 'to destroy [or, perhaps better, 'go beyond'] knowledge, in order to make room for faith': *Ich mußte also das Wissen aufheben, um zum Glauben Platz zu bekommen.*[18]

---

[17] *An Enquiry Concerning Human Nature*, Sectn XII, Part 1, §12.
[18] Kant, *Critique of Pure Reason*, B xxx.

But even if this interpretation is correct, Hume's killer argument has not quite been defused. Granted, the mystic need not (as Hume alleges) be an atheist without knowing it; but the second prong of Hume's critique still remains: is he or she really not a sceptic without knowing it? Is there really any substantial difference between devoutly and faithfully *believing* in a mysterious *x about which nothing can be known*, and being in a state of doubt or ignorance about whether there is any such *x*?

It seems quite clear that there is a difference. Let us take the example of causation once again. A Humean sceptic about causality presumably thinks there *may be* some secret, unknowable, underlying power responsible for all the correlations we observe in the physical world; though such a 'secret connexion', since it is *ex hypothesi* unobservable, must remain 'forever shut up from human curiosity and inquiry'. The crucial point about such a stance is clearly its complete *neutrality*. Such a sceptic has no basis for asserting that there *must* be, or even that there *probably* is, such an underlying unknown basis for observed correlations, any more than for asserting that there cannot be or that there probably is not such a basis. Our knowledge, being confined to the world of experience, is limited to the correlations, the 'constant conjunctions' we actually observe; and for all the sceptic knows, or is prepared to say, this *could* be all there is. In other words, as far as what actually exists or occurs is concerned, it could well be that there are just certain repeated regularities in the cosmos, and that is simply all there is to it. (Many 'regularity theorists' of causation, often thought of as Humeans, would say precisely that.) This, then, would be the properly worked out implication of the sceptical position about causality: we cannot know anything about any supposed underlying realities beyond the regular correlations we observe; and, for all we know, there may not *be* any.

The 'believer' about causal connections, by contrast, would be very different. Such a believer, we may suppose, is convinced, has a powerful conviction that he will not abandon, that there are, that there must be, secret connexions underlying the observed regularities in the world; yet he admits that he has no way of explaining, investigating or comprehending the nature of such realities. They are mysterious.

The parallel with religious belief seems clear. A sceptic, in the sense we are now considering, is one who suspends belief on whether there is any transcendent divine entity 'behind the scenes' – beyond the natural world. And in any case he regards any answer to such a question as beyond human knowledge. There is no way we can know whether there is a God. Epistemically, this is quite a modest or cautious position.

However, as popularly used (and as Hume may be using it in the passage we are discussing), the 'sceptical outlook' goes a bit further than mere suspension of belief: we often call someone sceptical not only when he thinks that nothing can be known about whether some given claim is true, but when he is pretty doubtful about its truth, or inclined to think it false. This is, if you like, a strong, or 'eyebrow raising', or 'frowning' sceptic, rather than just a 'shrugging the shoulders' sceptic. The strong sceptic, in addition to thinking supposed divine entities are forever beyond possible human knowledge, is actually pretty much inclined to believe that the world of experience is all there is, and that is that. The strong sceptic is thus strongly inclined to maintain that the cosmos we live in, the natural, observable world, is a 'closed' world: that a complete inventory of reality would include all the directly or indirectly observable objects of experience and nothing else. (Such a 'strong sceptic' is pretty close to the kind of 'naturalism' that has become so prevalent in the current philosophical establishment.)

The mystic, the believer in a divine reality beyond our comprehension, is clearly, *pace* Hume, quite different from this. He or she clearly differs from the strong, 'frowning' sceptic or naturalist, because he or she believes that the cosmos is *not* closed: it owes its being to a transcendent reality that cannot be included in the complete inventory of natural objects and events. But he also differs from the weaker or more neutral (shoulder shrugging) sceptic: the mystic is strongly committed, as a matter of faith, to the existence of such a transcendent being, while at the same time acknowledging that we do not and cannot comprehend its nature.

3. The problems of transcendence

Hume's challenge to the mystic, at any rate as he puts it, thus does not succeed. The mystic is not an atheist without knowing it, and he is not a sceptic, either in the strong or the weak sense, without knowing it. Nevertheless, although it technically fails, I do think that Hume's remark succeeds in highlighting a major problem for the believer who invokes (as many philosophers of religion do) the complete transcendence or 'otherness' of God. For such a move seems to place the deity so far beyond our reach that we are denied any basis for considering him a proper object of *worship*. Hume's acid observation that the mystic regards God as '*adorably* mysterious' brings this nicely into focus. How can something be an object of adoration if its nature is beyond anything we can conceive?

Those actually involved in mystical religious praxis do not seem to be too bothered by this kind of worry. Thomas Merton, following in a long line of spiritual writers in the apophatic tradition, puts his creed as follows:

> He who is infinite light is so tremendous in His evidence that our minds only see Him as darkness. *Lux in tenebris lucet et tenebrae eam non comprehendunt* ['The light shines in the darkness, and the darkness does not comprehend it', John 1:5]. If nothing that can be seen can either be God or represent Him to us as He is, then to find God we must pass beyond everything that can be seen and enter into darkness. Since nothing that can be heard is God, to find Him we must enter into silence . . . God cannot be understood except by Himself. If we are to understand Him we can only do so by being in some way transformed into Him, so that we may know him as He knows Himself. Faith is the first step in this transformation because it is a cognition that knows without images and representations by a loving identification with the living God in obscurity.[19]

---

[19] Thomas Merton, *Seeds of Contemplation* [1961], Ch. 19, 'From Faith to Wisdom'. Cf. Turner, *The Darkness of God* [1995], for a more philosophical treatment.

This may be too paradoxical for many people's taste, but it does go at least some way to circumventing objections of a Humean kind. The point is not to attempt to determine the nature of God but to reach out and seek him in love. Descending into darkness and silence is a kind of acknowledgement that there is nothing for the believer to *say* that can specify the content of his belief, or separate him out, in cognitive terms, from the non-believer or the sceptic; but there is something he *does*, namely devote himself in silence and humility and faith to being open to an intimation that cannot be put into words.

Merton's position is not intended to be evaluated as an abstract argument, but is better understood as an invitation to involvement in a certain kind of spiritual praxis. But others have recently tried to provide a more abstract defence of the apophatic approach, by claiming that it is not only nothing to be philosophically embarrassed about, but is in fact the hallmark of a sound theology. The contemporary philosopher of religion, Jean-Luc Marion, has argued that we need to abandon entirely the standard theological attempt to characterize the nature or essence of God. For example, referring to God as the original 'cause' of everything in no way names God, says Marion; rather, it '*de-nominates* him by suggesting the strictly pragmatic function of language – namely to refer names and their speaker to the unattainable yet inescapable interlocutor beyond every name and every denegation of names'.[20] The attempt to determine the 'essence' or 'nature' of the ineffable

---

20 Jean-Luc Marion, 'In the Name', in J. Caputo and M. Scanlon, *God, The Gift and Postmodernism* [1999], p. 27.

God is, on this view, simply a form of idolatry. St Anselm's famous formulation in his ontological argument might be invoked as support: God is not the 'greatest conceivable being', but is *id quo nihil maius cogitari potest* – 'that than which nothing greater can be thought'.[21] Like a necessarily receding horizon, God eludes the limits of our thought, so that any claim to bring him within the horizon of our cognition would be self-refuting: the purported achievement would be the best possible evidence that what had been brought within the horizon was not God, but a lesser being, a mere 'god' – an idol. Marion eloquently sums up his position as follows:

> God cannot be seen, not only because nothing finite can bear his glory without perishing, but above all because a God that could be conceptually comprehended would no longer bear the title 'God'. It is not much to say that God remains God even if one is ignorant of his essence, his concept, and his presence – he remains God only on condition that this ignorance be established and admitted definitively. Every thing in the world gains by being known – but God who is not of the world, gains by not being known conceptually. The idolatry of the concept is the same as that of the gaze, imagining oneself to have attained God and to be capable of maintaining him under our gaze, like a thing of the world. And the Revelation of God consists first of all in cleaning the slate of this illusion and its blasphemy.[22]

---

21 Anselm of Canterbury, *Proslogion* [1077–8], Ch. 2.

22 Marion, 'In the Name', p. 34.

The avoidance of blasphemy is a worthy enough aim, and the warning against subjecting God to our 'gaze' harmonizes with the ancient injunction (observed in Judaism and Islam) which prohibits making images of God or representing him pictorially. But despite its appeal, Marion's position risks sliding into incoherence, for the kind of reason I have already hinted at. Marion's language, like Merton's, is the language of worship, of awe. That this incomprehensible being is one to whom we should respond by speaking of his 'glory', or needing to seek him in devotion, makes no sense unless we have some sense of a being who is *personal* – an 'interlocutor', as Marion puts it, or someone with whom, in Merton's words, we can seek a 'loving identification'. What is logically implied by such personal language is that God can be characterized in predicates or properties that are drawn from human experience, or at least analogous to something drawn from human experience. But if that is right, then the apophatic premise that God is entirely transcendent, to be apprehended only in complete 'ignorance', cannot stand. The mystic, in short, cannot have it both ways. Either the apophatic approach is maintained intact, in which case mysticism cannot offer us a valid object of religious worship; or else worship is retained as appropriate, in which case the apophatic approach is eroded, and there has to be at least something that can be validly said of God.

How, if at all, can the theist avoid these problems, stemming from the traditional doctrine of the transcendence or otherness of God? One possible solution is the one which the Dutch–Jewish philosopher Benedict Spinoza developed in the seventeenth century: to cut the Gordian knot, and to deny divine transcendence in the first place. Spinoza's God, what he called *Deus sive Natura* ('God or Nature'), is immanent in the world, indeed identical with the world. There is a single substance, which can be conceived either 'under the attribute of thought' (as active mind) or 'under the attribute of extension' (as the physical world).[23] Evaluating such immanentism would take us too far away from our main theme; but it may be worth indicating briefly some of its problems. In the first place, it is no accident that Spinoza repudiated the possibility of revelation: there can be no supernatural intervention given the Spinozan worldview because there is nothing supernatural.[24] Spinozism is (at least on its most plausible reading) a form of naturalism, and, along with contemporary naturalism, maintains a 'closed' cosmos, a cosmos that is autonomous and necessarily sealed off from any possible action of a transcendent creative power. So it is also no accident that Spinozism was regarded among Spinoza's contemporaries and successors as the royal road to atheism. From a religious perspective, to be sure, it does claim to offer a kind of 'loving identification' (to revert to Merton's term) – what Spinoza famously called the *amor intellectualis Dei*, the 'intellectual love of God'.[25] Yet it turns out that that love cannot be anything individual or

---

[23] Benedict Spinoza, *Ethics* [1665], Part I. For an exposition of Spinoza's views and their background, see Cottingham, *The Rationalists* [1988], Ch. 2.

[24] See, for example, the denial of Spinoza's treatment of miracles in the *Tractatus Theologico-Politicus* [1670]. For Spinoza's (somewhat idiosyncratic) account of 'revelation', within a naturalistic framework, see Alan Donagan, 'Spinoza's Theology', in D. Garrett (ed.), *The Cambridge Companion to Spinoza*, Ch. 8.

[25] Spinoza, *Ethics*, Part V.

personal, but amounts instead to a calm sense of the totality of the inevitable process of which each of us is a fleeing modification. Its mindset is most reminiscent of the Stoic creed of Marcus Aurelius: 'In the thought that I am part of the whole, I shall be content with all that can come to pass';[26] or perhaps with the Buddhist impersonalism that takes comfort from the thought that conditions arise and pass away, and I am not a genuine Self, but simply a temporary locus of certain kinds of change. This is not to say that it is not a creed with many attractions, or that it is not entitled to be called, in a certain sense, religious. But it diverges too far from anything recognizably theistic to be a candidate for a solution to the kind of problem which Hume posed for theism.

4. Revelation and the Incarnate Word

The general lesson we have drawn from considering Hume's remarks about mystical and transcendent theism is that the theist needs to avoid placing God so far beyond the reach of human understanding that he ceases to become a valid object of religious worship. So the practical requirements of the worshipper, and the philosophical concerns of the Enlightenment about the limits of human understanding, converge on a single point: the need for a bridge between the transcendent and the experiential, a bridge between the divine and the human. This is of course precisely what is offered by the Christian doctrine of the Incarnation. Someone of a sceptical Humean cast of

---

[26] Marcus Aurelius, *Meditations* [*c*. AD 85], VI, 42.

mind would probably be inclined to say that invoking the Incarnation looks like attempting to repair the flaws in transcendent theistic mysticism by wheeling in yet another incomprehensible mystery – the mystery of God made man. Yet the bridging, the translation, as it were, of the ineffable and incomprehensible divine nature into something accessible to human experience, does have a certain internal logic. It is a logic well expressed by the poet Gerard Manley Hopkins, who compares the transcendent God, dwelling in light inaccessible, to the brightness of the sun, which would destroy us utterly unless it were 'sifted' by the Earth's blue envelope of atmosphere – a metaphor for the Virgin Mary, through whom God's ineffable glory becomes incarnate:

> Whereas, did air not make
> This bath of blue, and slake
> His fire, the sun would shake
> A blear and blinding ball . . .

> So God was God of old:
> A mother came to mould
> Those limbs like ours which are
> What must make our daystar
> Much dearer to mankind;
> Whose glory bare would blind . . .[27]

---

[27] Gerard Manley Hopkins, 'The Blessed Virgin Compared to the Air We Breath', from *Poems (1876–1889)*.

God's glory, blinding, incomprehensible, transcendent, can nonetheless become known to humanity, and reach into our lives, but only if it is 'sifted to suit our sight'. Translated, as it were, into human terms, it can make itself both visible, and also, in taking human flesh, 'much dearer to mankind' – a pattern of goodness for us to follow, 'full of grace and truth', an object of our love and devotion.

That an idea is beautiful, that it answers to our restless human need to know God, does not, of course, make it true. And attempts to *prove* it true – for example by claiming that the genuineness of the Incarnation is certified by miracles (the star in the east, for example, or the angelic announcement to the shepherds) – seem doomed to fail, for reasons of the kind Hume himself so eloquently deployed elsewhere, in the First Enquiry.[28] From a neutral, scientific standpoint, assessing the records coolly on the basis of empirical probabilities, it is hard to see how the available evidence could stack up in favour of the authenticity of such reported signs and wonders; and there is in any case something bizarre about the idea of looking for purely scientific evidence for the conclusion that God became man at a certain point in history – the very paradigm of a *magnum mysterium*, a 'great and mighty wonder'.[29] Only for one who already has faith in God will the Incarnation appear

---

[28] David Hume, *An Enquiry Concerning Human Understanding* [1748], Section X, Part 2.

[29] From the ancient responsorial chant for Christmas Day: *O magnum mysterium et admirabile sacramentum, ut animalia viderent Dominum natum jacentem in praesepio* ('O great mystery and wonderful sacrament, that animals should see the new-born Lord, lying in a manger!').

to be even a candidate for something that might 'reasonably' have been supposed to occur.[30] So it seems misguided to look for some independent, non-circular justification for accepting that Jesus Christ was, in Paul's phrase, an 'icon of the invisible God' (Colossians 1:15). Acceptance that this human being was indeed a unique manifestation of the divine – that his life and teachings, displayed in human terms that we can understand, provide us with a definitive route to the incomprehensible and transcendent creator – is something that must remain in large measure dependent on faith. For Hume, this only serves to underline the unsatisfactory nature of the whole thing. As he says at the end of Section X of the *First Enquiry*: 'The Christian religion not only was at first attended with miracles, but even at this day cannot be believed by any reasonable person without one.'[31] But the believer is unlikely to be crushed by this cutting irony. Standard Christian orthodoxy, it is true, has always understood faith as a gift bestowed by God, and hence as dependent on supernatural grace. But this does not mean it is irrational or absurd. An act of will may be required to open oneself to the process, but many of the Church fathers argued that this is quite compatible with subsequent intellectual assent. Faith can 'seek understanding',[32] and (as we shall suggest

---

30 Contrast the reasoned probabilistic approach taken in R. Swinburne, *Was Jesus God?* [2008].

31 Hume, *Enquiry Concerning Human Understanding*, Section X, Part 2, penultimate paragraph.

32 Compare Aquinas: 'believing is an act of the intellect assenting to the divine truth on the basis of a command of the will moved by God through grace, and so it is subject to free choice of the will in its being ordered toward God. That is why the act of faith can be meritorious.' (Aquinas, *Summa theologiae*

in Chapter 5), supporting evidence may become available once we put ourselves in a position which allows us to be receptive to it.

Yet what of someone who does not yet believe, but who is on the threshold, or is at least a possible candidate for a believer? Talk of the need to open oneself to divine grace may be all very well, but such language is unlikely to mean very much except to those already within the religious belief-system. To those outside, the call for receptivity and openness may seem like an invitation to self-surrender which they see no reason to accept – all the more so if they have suspicions that the belief-system they would be asked to adopt may not qualify as rational or reasonable in the first place. One cannot step over the threshold if it is blocked in advance. It will be the task of our next chapter to examine some of the principal obstacles to belief.

[1266–73], IIaIIae 2, 9). The idea of 'faith seeking understanding' (*fides quaerens intellectum*) is found in Anselm's *Proslogion*.

Chapter 4

Obstacles to Belief

Our Sun is a star, one among millions, in fact part way out within one arm of a galaxy . . . Consider then the claim. We are being asked to believe, are we, to put it crudely, that God put in an appearance on planet earth? The mind boggles.

Daphne Hampson[1]

1. How difficult can it get?

It is surprisingly common for contemporary theologians, and religious apologists generally, to open their discussions by observing how *hard* it is, in our modern world, to believe in God, or to accept the tenets of Christianity. They may intend to reach a more positive note by the end of the argument, but in a climate of short attention spans it is the opening negative impression that tends to stick. Their stance is reminiscent of the story of a distinguished professor whose job was to recruit first-year undergraduates to sign up for philosophy courses. He would begin: 'You may have heard that philosophy is a

---

[1] Daphne Hampson, *After Christianity* [2002], p. 30.

difficult subject, that it is *very abstract*, that it is *not much help in earning a living*, that it requires *demanding logical skills . . .*' His plan was to get all the possible obstacles out of the way, before coming on to highlight some more alluring aspects of the subject; but as he got into his stride, expatiating on the reasons that might influence someone to *avoid* philosophy, a clear idea began to form itself in the minds of his student listeners: 'That subject is not for me!' By the time he got round to the arguments in favour of philosophy, the audience had made up their minds, and the positive case arrived too late to do much good.

The Gospel reading for the Feast of the Transfiguration describes Jesus taking Peter, James and John up to a 'high mountain' where they saw his face 'become bright as the sun, and his clothes as white as light' (Matthew 17). In a recent sermon on this text, the preacher opened by saying, 'I've always found this a very *difficult* episode.' The faintly embarrassed tone is familiar from a long history of awkward retreat among clerics, which goes back to the advent of 'modern' biblical criticism, the aim of which was to subject the Bible to the kind of dispassionate scrutiny that any professional historian would show towards source materials. Well-meaning, anxious not to appear out of date or unscientific, often genuinely worried about the plausibility of some of the episodes recorded in scripture, the exponents of this style of theology will bracket off as fictitious one reported miraculous event after another: the water turned into wine must be merely symbolic or illustrative; the feeding of the five thousand with five loaves and two fishes must be exaggerated (perhaps an illustration of what can be achieved by people pooling their limited food under the influence of a powerful moral leader); the Transfiguration, not a historical event but part of a pattern of interpretation imposed by a subsequent 'high Christology'; the healing miracles either attributable to suggestibility or the placebo effect, or else pure inventions the purpose of which is to show Jesus as the last and greatest of the prophets; the Virgin Birth and the other Nativity stories an exercise in myth-making, bearing little relation to the likely historical circumstances of Jesus's birth. Curiously, the Resurrection often tends to be exempted from this process – a last bastion whose historicity many theologians are reluctant to abandon, at any rate in the pulpit, and sometimes even in the seminar room, perhaps out of fear that once Jesus of Nazareth is reduced to a mere man and nothing more, there will be no logical reason for keeping God in the story at all.

But even this final bullet has now long since been bitten, for example by the theologian Don Cupitt, in his significantly titled *Taking Leave of God*, which offered a 'fully demythologized version of Christianity', and explicitly abandoned the idea of religious faith as grounded in anything beyond the natural and the human realms.[2] Cupitt's book followed in the wake of a naturalizing movement in theology, which had enjoyed a long history, harking back to the demythologizing agenda advocated by earlier theologians such as Rudolf Bultmann (with origins that go back as far as Spinoza in the

---

2 Don Cupitt, *Taking Leave of God* [1980]. See also Chapter 1, above, footnote 20.

seventeenth century).[3] The movement continues to enjoy widespread support, as may be seen in the following analysis of the Resurrection, by the distinguished present-day Professor of Theology, Ingolf Dalferth:

> Jesus [in Mark's Gospel] dedicated his entire 'career' to God's promise and counted on his faithfulness and support all the way to the cross, but in the end he was disappointed by God and died in despair . . . In Mark's story of Jesus . . . a dramatic conflict is built up between Jesus' understanding of God as proclaimed in the gospel and the loss of God by the proclaimer of that gospel as he dies on the cross. This conflict is not resolved in the gospel narrative of his life, but – the account of the empty grave (Mk 16, 1–8) and the secondary ending of Mark (Mk 16, 9–20) substantiate this – *finds resolution only in the life of those to whom this story is told* and who experience the crucified as the resurrected one. The darkness into which the understanding of God falls on the cross is lifted and repealed *not in the life story of Jesus, and therefore for Jesus himself,* but in the life story of those who believe in him as Christ, and therefore for others.[4]

---

3 R. K. Bultmann, 'Neues Testament und Mythologie' [1941]. For an insightful discussion of Bultmann's naturalistic presuppositions, see Douglas Hedley, *Living Forms of the Imagination* [2008], Ch. 4. For Spinoza, see Ch. 3, Section 3, above.

4 Ingolf Dalferth, 'Self-Sacrifice: From the Act of Violence to the Passion of Love' [2008], p. 9, emphasis added.

There appears (on Dalferth's interpretation) to be no actual resurrection, since there is no renewal of life in Jesus himself; all that happens is that those around him are able to 'experience him *as* the resurrected one' (emphasis added). But why, in that case, should the language of Jesus being 'raised' by God not be discarded altogether? On the suggested interpretation, is not the message of the Gospels reduced to no more than an inspiring moral lesson about love and self-sacrifice? Dalferth himself (unlike Cupitt) seems not quite ready to dispense with talk of God entirely; for at the end of the paper he insists that the life and death of Jesus gets its meaning through being an 'irreversible sign that here God discloses himself as unselfish, unconditional love'. He goes on: 'This is why [Christians] confess Jesus as God's love incarnate, and God's love as his creative presence that creates good out of evil and new possibilities for his creatures even in death. *Even where they themselves cannot realize this any more, others will.*'[5]

Yet if one takes the talk of God's 'creative presence' seriously, then one wonders why it needs to be construed in a way that makes it so comparatively inefficacious. Why is it that the 'creation of good out of evil' can only take the form of possible future actions by others once the main protagonists have died? There is perhaps something vaguely inspiring about the thought that there will always be future possibilities for loving self-sacrifice, but one wonders whether this can really be what Christians are celebrating at Easter – the fact that Jesus himself, and those who followed him in the path of love, saw their own

---

[5] Dalferth, 'Self-Sacrifice', p. 10; emphasis added.

struggles end in death and despair, but that in spite of this others may be able to carry on the struggle? The rousing Easter hymns which generations have sung to affirm Christ's triumph over death would come out as pallid and forlorn shadows of themselves if put through this naturalistic sieve.

The point of these remarks is not at all to disparage the scholarship or the sincerity of theological writing such as Dalferth's, but rather to highlight the dilemma facing the defender of Christianity in a scientific age (and a similar impasse evidently confronts the defender of Judaism or Islam, in so far as both religions, in their traditional form, are committed to the idea of divine intervention into the natural course of history). Either, it seems, one can take the naturalistic and 'demythologizing' route pioneered by Bultmann (and Spinoza before him), or else one can become a 'hardliner', insisting, come what may, on the literal truth of various supernatural interventions as recorded in scripture. Yet the former route risks draining the lifeblood from religious praxis and worship – why joyfully celebrate the wonderful saving actions of God, if the recorded episodes did not in fact actually occur? – and perhaps sooner or later leads to the very idea of God losing any decisive foothold in our belief system. The latter route, by contrast, retreats to the seemingly secure stronghold of traditional faith and worship, but at what appears to be a very severe cost – that of saddling us with the kind of rigid 'Take it or leave it' fundamentalism that simply closes the door to any contact with the modern scientific age.

So how hard can it get? Has traditional religious belief really become so difficult, in our modern scientific world, that the only intellectually respectable way forward is to drain it of any reference to supernatural agency? Or do we abandon the attempt to reconcile religious belief with modern science and withdraw to the redoubt of fundamentalism? Or (a third possibility), might the dilemma itself be misconceived – might the clash between science and scripture turn out after all to be resolvable? Let us retrace our steps and try to see a way forward through this tangle.

2. Supernatural intervention

In its bluntest form, the question that faces contemporary believers, or would-be believers, is whether they are prepared to countenance the idea of supernatural intervention. The believer does not, of course, have to go to the stake for each and every supposedly miraculous event reported in scripture, but however many of the biblical stories are finessed or explained away, there will remain a core of reported episodes the genuineness of which has always been regarded as absolutely central to the faith. Such events surely include, for Christians or prospective Christians, the Resurrection of Christ, which on any interpretation seems to be a cornerstone of Christianity. Unlike most of the other miraculous occurrences in the New Testament, it is unequivocally affirmed in all three Christian Creeds,[6] and it has a foundational status for the faith[7] –

---

[6] The Apostles' Creed (whose origins go back to the first century AD), the Nicene Creed (AD 325) and the Athanasian Creed (fifth century).

[7] Compare Paul: 'If Christ be not raised, your faith is vain', 1 Corinthians 15:17.

comparable to the disclosure of the Law to Moses in Judaism, or of the Qur'an to Mohammed in Islam. What is more, it is a paradigm of a miraculous episode, in the strong sense of something quite contrary to the natural course of events. Ordinary human experience, repeated day in, day out, century after century, confirms that people do not revive after being clinically dead for over 24 hours;[8] and (as Hume famously pointed out)[9] the weight of empirical evidence must therefore, by the very nature of the supposed event, be stacked against the veracity of the scriptural claim that it actually occurred.

But does science really rule out the Resurrection? To many modern theologians, the answer is a clear affirmative. Thus John Macquarrie writes:

> The way of understanding miracles that appeals to breaks in the natural order and to supernatural intervention belongs to the mythological outlook and cannot commend itself in a post-mythological climate of thought . . . The traditional conception of miracle is irreconcilable with our modern understanding of both science and history. Science proceeds on the assumption that whatever events occur in the world can be accounted for in

---

[8] The period, from late on Friday to very early on Sunday morning, is not much more than this. The point is worth making because the English rendering of the Latin phrase from the Creed, *tertio die* ('on the third day'), is misleading. The Greeks and Romans, unlike us, counted their days inclusively, so a better (if less literal) translation into modern English would be 'on the second day', or 'after an interval of one day'.

[9] David Hume, *An Enquiry Concerning Human Understanding* [1748], Section X.

terms of other events that also belong within the world; and if on some occasions we are unable to give a complete account of some happening . . . the scientific conviction is that further research will bring to light further factors in the situation, but factors that will turn out to be just as immanent and this-worldly as those already known.[10]

There is no doubt that many scientists and laypeople would agree with this resolute refusal to countenance 'breaks in the natural order'. But there is a crucial ambiguity in Macquarrie's formulation. He is surely right to say that science 'proceeds on the assumption' that whatever happens in the world is to be explained naturalistically ('in terms of other events that also belong within the world'). But what is the status of this assumption? Construed one way, it is simply a *methodological recommendation*: that science should always continue the search for natural explanations. Such 'methodological naturalism' (as we may call it) is clearly part of our modern scientific framework – and, one may add, it has turned out to be extremely fruitful in encouraging scientists to seek for natural physical causes of otherwise mysterious or baffling phenomena. But there is another way of understanding the 'assumption' referred to by Macquarrie, namely as a *metaphysical principle*: that there are, and can be, no other causes beyond those contained within the natural world. Construed this way, the principle amounts to an insistence that the universe is a closed system – impermeable, as

10 John Macquarrie, *Principles of Christian Theology* [1977], p. 248.

it were, to any possible supernatural influence; or, if you prefer, a complete self-contained totality such that no putative 'outside' influence is even conceivable. Now, of course the universe may indeed be 'closed' in this way: the complete set of physical events since the Big Bang, and all the various properties and occurrences arising out of those events, may comprise absolutely everything that there is. But such a claim is clearly a piece of metaphysics, not a piece of science. Since science, by definition, deals only with 'immanent and this-worldly' phenomena (in Macquarrie's phrase), it could never establish the truth of this kind of metaphysical claim. No scientific procedure could conceivably establish that there is or can be nothing that transcends the natural world.

Suppose for the sake of argument that the basic thesis of traditional theism is true – that there is a supreme, supernatural being, who created and conserves the entire fabric of the natural world. Suppose that the total set of events from the Big Bang onwards was brought into existence by the will of God – that, as the fourth Gospel has it, 'all things were made by him, and without him was not anything made that was made'. On the assumption of such a being, would the idea of 'breaks in the natural order' be untenable and unscientific? Clearly not: for on the assumption we are considering, the cosmos is *not* closed, but was brought into being and sustained by an outside influence; so, on this picture there would be nothing intrinsically odd about the idea of supernatural irruptions into the natural order. Science *qua* the study of natural phenomena would simply have to remain silent about this possibility.

Putting the matter this way may seem to beg the question

against the naturalist by assuming the existence of a super-natural being who might intervene in the world. But it is important to see that *even on a purely naturalist worldview*, even without bringing God into the picture, the categorical assertion that there can be no 'breaks' in the natural order is unwarranted. Consider for instance the standard system of classical physics based on Newtonian principles. As the eminent contemporary philosopher of religion Alvin Plantinga points out, 'Energy is conserved in a closed system; but it is not part of Newtonian mechanics of classical science generally to declare that the material universe is indeed a closed system. (How could such a claim possibly be verified experimentally?)'[11] The impossibility of breaks in the natural order follows not from Newtonian science on its own, but only from Newtonian science *plus* the additional declaration that the natural universe is a causally closed system. Yet that last declaration is no part of Newtonian (or any other) science.

Modern quantum physics has of course departed in important respects from the Newtonian model, and now construes events at the micro level in a probabilistic, not a deterministic, fashion. But this means that the alleged scientific impossibility of 'breaks in the natural order' is even less well supported. In an indeterministic universe, a complete specification of the present state of the universe will not enable us to deduce its future state, but only to calculate the probability of particular future states occurring: 'We must take as the best assumption

---

[11] See Alvin Plantinga, 'Divine Action in the World: Synopsis' [2006].

that the world is essentially probabilistic.'[12] If such indeterminism is indeed an inherent feature of the physical universe, as many interpreters of modern physics maintain, then it appears that we are in no position to rule out the occurrence of events quite contrary to the normally observed regularities; someone's walking on water, for example, will not strictly be physically impossible, merely extremely improbable.

The upshot is that modern science, irrespective of whether we are talking about classical or quantum physics, is in no position to rule out breaks in the natural order. From a purely scientific point of view, there can be no rational basis for declaring the Resurrection, or any other miracles, to be absolutely out of court.

In the light of this, if there are to be any decisive objections against supernatural intervention, it seems they would have to come from a theological or an ethical rather than a scientific quarter. It might, for example, be thought objectionable that God, having set up the regularities of nature, would then violate them. But this objection clearly does not stand up. If a regular pattern of natural occurrences depends ultimately on the will of a rational being, then there is clearly no 'violation' involved in his deciding to act in such a way that the regularity in question breaks down, or is suspended. (If someone regularly goes for a walk at three o'clock every afternoon, there need be no objectionable 'violation' of regularity involved in her deciding to stay at home one afternoon in order to tend to a sick member of the household; she has merely acted differently

---

12 W. H. Newton-Smith, *The Rationality of Science* [1981], p. 222.

from the usual pattern, and that is that.) Or again, another objection might be drawn from the supposed perfection and immutability of God: if God operates (as traditional theology insists he does) in an absolutely constant and unchangeable way, then is it not a contradiction to think of his altering the behaviour of the natural world in response to particular circumstances? But this kind of worry need not detain defenders of divine intervention for long: following a standard line in the theological literature, they will reply that God is not to be thought of as 'changing his mind', or 'acting out of character', but rather as eternally decreeing that a certain unusual event will come about precisely on the occasion of some special set of circumstances. In the end, the only plausibly worrying philosophical objection to the idea of divine intervention seems to boil down to an ethical complaint against his justice or benevolence: if God does indeed have the power and inclination to intervene in the normal natural order of events (for example, so as to raise someone from the dead), then, given that he is supposed to be loving and benevolent, how can one explain his failure to intervene in so many *other* cases of death, undeserved suffering and human misery? The problem of the suffering of the innocent is, to be sure, a notoriously vexed theological issue (one we shall be returning to in our final chapter); but it takes us into entirely different territory from the supposed difficulty or impossibility of divine intervention as such.

The conclusion of this part of the argument must be that those many theologians who have agonized over developing a scientifically up-to-date theology (or quasi-theology), one which dispenses with divine intervention in the natural world, have been struggling to respond to a supposed problem that does not in fact exist. The respect such theologians show for the modern scientific worldview is commendable; but their conception of what that worldview excludes is philosophically confused. Nothing in science does, or can, rule out the possibility of divine intervention. To be sure, if we do, after all, live in a wholly natural and entirely 'closed' cosmos, then there is no such thing as a supernatural realm, and *a fortiori* no supernatural intervention. But *that* question, however it is to be settled, cannot be decided on the basis of anything disclosed by modern science.

3. Back to fundamentalism?

If the door to supernatural intervention thus remains open, is the way clear for a return to literalism and fundamentalism in scriptural interpretation? Some of those who are understandably suspicious of the naturalizing tendency in modern liberal theology might be tempted to welcome such a result; but many considerations suggest that it is not the right way forward.

In the first place, the message from the previous section, that the modern scientific framework is formally compatible with the idea of divine intervention into the natural order, needs to be understood correctly. Nothing in science, as we have seen, strictly rules out the possibility of a supernatural order which might in some way impinge on the natural order. But to make sense of this conclusion we need to have a proper idea of what the natural order amounts to in the first place. And to do that, we cannot ignore the achievements of modern science. There can be no doubt that the last two or three centuries – the gradually unfolding era of what is known as the 'scientific revolution' – have seen a vast array of highly successful, and purely naturalistic, explanations of phenomena formerly thought by many to be of supernatural origin. When Descartes and Galileo laid the foundations for the new mathematical physics in the seventeenth century, they inaugurated a framework of enormous power and scope that has very largely delivered on its promises for a comprehensive and systematic method of understanding the entire universe. We should not want to throw away that achievement, or go back on it, even if we could.

The world of our distant ancestors was a frightening, uncontrollable world, animated by gods and spirits whose capricious actions were thought responsible for storms and droughts, plenty and famine, thunder and earthquakes, fertility and sterility, and all the other vicissitudes of our precarious human existence. It was a world of fear and superstition, which no one should feel nostalgic about. The slowly developing frameworks of rational inquiry that emerged in the culture of the classical and medieval periods were vastly more sophisticated than this primitive animism; but in trying to come to terms with the world, they were still reduced in many cases to a haphazard and piecemeal array of methods and concepts, many of which were lacking in any true explanatory power. Writing as late as 1581, the Renaissance philosopher and medical writer Francisco Sanches records with devastating frankness the extent to which he was trapped in the inescapable ignorance of the pre-Enlightenment world. Whenever he canvasses possible routes to knowledge, he can only rehearse a ramshackle conventional apparatus of 'qualities and form, sympathies and antipathies', with no notion of what might be used to replace it: 'Blackness may be produced by heat (as with the Ethiopians) or from cold (as in a gangrened limb); heat may be produced by cold (as when lime is slaked in cold water); cold from heat (as when hot bodies are consumed by fire) and also in the Ethiopians, who are cold inside (and so are we, in summer) . . .' So it goes on, a rambling catalogue illuminated only by the honest realization that no materials are to hand which could merit the title of genuine understanding of the world around us: *Misera est conditio nostra. In media luce coecutimus* ('Wretched is our condition; in the midst of light we are blind').[13]

The early-modern and Enlightenment philosophers and scientists, by contrast, were able to develop a research programme of supreme simplicity and elegance: all the workings of nature were to be understood using the clear and distinct concepts of mathematics, and the theories formulated in this way were to be checked against careful observation. Descartes, in his triumphant advocacy of the new quantitative approach, envisaged an 'unbroken chain' which links together seemingly diverse phenomena, such as light and heat, magnetism and fire, clouds and vapours, plants and animals; the 'long chains of reasoning' of the mathematicians were to be a model for the way in which 'all the items which fall within the scope of human knowledge are interconnected'.[14] And he concluded

---

[13] Francisco Sanches, *That Nothing is Known* [1581], ed. D. Thomson, p. 243.
[14] *Discourse* [1637], Part 2.

with confidence (a confidence that history has largely vindicated) that there are 'no properties of magnets and of fire which are so amazing . . . no powers in stones or plants that are so mysterious, no marvels attributed to sympathetic or antipathetic influences that are so astonishing that they cannot be explained in this way'.[15]

It is important to appreciate the grandeur and magnificence of the modern scientific enterprise. Its spectacular success means that there is no putting the clock back, no possibility of a return to an animistic or mythological framework for understanding the world. But where does this leave religion? Some religious believers of a fundamentalist stamp give the impression of wanting to jump back in time, and insist that the world we inhabit is not, after all, the world disclosed by modern science, but a world capable of being magically manipulated by tapping into supernatural forces. There are those, for example, who maintain that the biblical story that the Lord made the sun stand still in the sky to give Joshua time to win a battle (Joshua 10:13) must be construed literally. But this is a prime example of a supposed event (the planet stops rotating for a few hours) that simply 'does not compute' within the modern way of thinking about the world. By this I do not mean that such an event is logically impossible, or beyond the powers of a supreme, all-powerful being to bring about. The mistake made by those who insist on taking such stories literally seems to me of a rather different order. It is the mistake of construing divine interventions as quasi-magical, para-scientific occurrences that

---

15 *Principles of Philosophy* [1644], Part IV, art. 187.

are enacted for the benefit of the chosen few (the believers), who have access to advantages or privileges denied to others. The kind of mindset involved here is typified by the pronouncements one sometimes hears from a certain type of staunchly fundamentalist believer: 'The LORD gave my rival a flat tyre so he would be late for the appointment and I would get the job.' 'Rain was forecast for the day of our garden party, but I prayed to the LORD, and he gave us a wonderful sunny day.'

To avoid misunderstanding, an important caveat needs to be entered at this point: I do not mean here to disparage all expressions of thankfulness to God for happy outcomes, still less to suggest that God never answers prayers.[16] What these examples are intended to draw attention to, instead, is the seductive but ultimately untenable conception of divine intervention as an *alternative mechanism* – available to the believer as a short cut (or perhaps as a 'fingers crossed' backup), to be used in addition, or in preference, to more conventional scientific or technological means of furthering one's projects. Such a con-

---

[16] The question of the efficacy of petitionary prayer is a vexed one to which there are no easy answers. I will simply say that a probabilistic approach to testing it (e.g. in the recent experiments in the USA where the cure rate of hospital patients prayed for was compared with that of a control group) appears to me to be misguided. The right kind of theological and philosophical framework for a solution seems much more likely to be contained in the following: 'It is time to reaffirm the importance of prayer in the face of . . . growing secularism . . . Clearly, the Christian who prays does not claim to be able to change God's plans or correct what he has foreseen. Rather, he seeks an encounter with the Father of Jesus Christ, asking God to be present with the consolation of the Spirit to him and his work.' Benedict XVI, *Deus Caritas Est* [Encyclical letter, 2005], §37.

ception appears to be ethically dubious (invoking God as a convenient resource for getting what one wants); and it also appears to involve an element of idolatry, for reasons that are graphically brought out in an essay by Herbert McCabe entitled 'The God of Truth':

> One way of starting to talk about the God of truth [is] to say a little about the gods of falsehood. It is characteristic of false gods that they are nothing but *objects of worship* . . . [W]orship of the gods often does contain an element of what you might call quasi-technology. If the forms and rites of worship are performed correctly in the traditional way, then certain results will ensue. The god will be propitiated and stop doing whatever nasty things it may be engaged in, like blighting the crops or withholding the rain or whatever. If it doesn't, you have got the ritual wrong. The gods are more powerful than we are, but they can be manipulated by presenting gifts of a kind they are known to like or by flattering their vanity and so on. For the gods, powerful as they are, are still fellow members of the universe. This indeed is the fundamental reason for *not* including the Creator (source of all being, truth and goodness) among the gods. For whatever else the creator might be . . . it cannot be a part of what it creates.[17]

How then *should* the believer understand the possibility of divine intervention? First of all, the action of God surely has to

---

17 H. McCabe, 'The God of Truth', in *God Still Matters* [2002], Ch. 3, pp. 29–30.

be conceived as operating against the background of the cosmos as we have it – the intricate, mathematically ordered dance of the largest galaxies and the smallest particles, the vast, complex interactive rhythm of the natural order, as it has unfolded over billions of years. This is the world disclosed by science – the world which even the most militant atheists will admit fills them with awe and wonder. And this picture, so far from being a *rival* to the theistic worldview, is strikingly compatible with it. The world we inhabit is, on any showing, a world of *reason*, of *logos* – a 'cosmos', in short, in the strict etymological sense of something that manifests *beauty and order*. Crude attempts (both by militant atheists and by dogmatic fundamentalists) to pitch science against religion completely miss the point here. Descartes, the champion and inaugurator of the new mathematical physics, was surely nearer the mark: for him, what is disclosed in the workings of the mathematical laws that govern the operation of the cosmos is not an *alternative* to God, but rather the creative intelligence of God himself.[18]

It could conceivably be, of course, that this intelligence unfolds coldly, impersonally, inexorably, without any particular interest in the fate of any conscious beings thrown up by the process, without any love or concern for us or those like us. That is the so-called 'deist' view (a view with which Descartes was – unjustly – saddled by Pascal[19]): the view of a God who

---

[18] For the passages in Descartes that support this (and some that suggest it needs some qualification), see J. Cottingham, *Cartesian Reflections* [2008], Ch. 15, §2.

[19] 'I cannot forgive Descartes: in all his philosophy he would have dispensed with God entirely, but he could not avoid allowing him a little shove [*chiquennaude*] to set the world in motion'. *Pensées* [*c.* 1660], ed. Lafuma, No. 1001.

sets the cosmos going, and perhaps keeps it in existence, but who takes no further interest in it or in its inhabitants. Yet pure reason isolated from concern in this way would be paradoxical, perhaps even ultimately absurd: it would be a personal characteristic cut off from the involvement that is inextricably bound up with the very idea of a personhood. 'Impersonal reason' is, in the end, a doubtfully coherent idea. There can of course be intelligent beings who take no interest in others – psychopaths, for example, or those suffering from extreme autism. But we rightly understand such people to be incomplete, deserving, in the former case, confinement, and, in the latter case, help and compassion. A being who is rational but whose purview cannot reach out to concern for others is but half a person, deficient even in certain basic attributes enjoyed by most humans, let alone qualifying for the supreme perfection that is inseparable from the concept of the divine. And so the dead-end of deism must give way to the joyful affirmation of traditional theism: that *logos* is identical with *agape*, that the divine reason is linked to concern, to mercy, to compassion, to love.

What would the interventions of such a creator be like? In affirming the loving nature of God, we are already partly in the area of faith, not philosophical reason alone,[20] so there must

---

[20] The reasoning of the previous paragraph (that rationality uncoupled from concern for others implies lack of perfection) might be combined with an Anselmian argument designed to show that God, defined as 'that than which nothing greater can be conceived', must be loving as well as powerful. I am, however, inclined to agree with (what I take to be) Anselm's own position, that such arguments are not free-standing philosophical arguments which might coerce the assent of any rational inquirer, but are rather exercises in 'faith seeking understanding' (Anselm of Canterbury, *Proslogion* [1077–8], Ch. 1).

inevitably be something presumptuous about trying to answer this question using the tools of philosophical argument. But even from the very minimalist characterization of God so far introduced, it seems plain that divine interventions could not be capricious exercises of power, nor convenient responses to the would-be manipulations of believers. Rather, they would necessarily be expressions of God's characteristics: they would be not arbitrary, but rational and intelligible; they would be not mere conferring of temporary advantages to one favourite as against another, or rewards for the performance of some mechanical ritual, but true manifestations of deep love and goodness. Perhaps most important, they would be *communications* between God and his creatures: they would be *disclosures of meaning*.

4. Revelation and recognition

The idea of a 'disclosure of meaning' provides what seems a particularly apt framework for approaching the supposedly 'difficult' story of the Transfiguration with which we began this chapter. This episode is clearly an extraordinary event in what was by any standards an extraordinary life, so one does not want to scale down its momentousness. But with that important proviso in place, the reported episode seems to have at least something in common with those 'transcendent' moments that many people will from time to time have experienced, the times when the drab, mundane pattern of our ordinary routines gives way to something vivid and radiant, and we seem to glimpse something of the significance of the world we inhabit. As Wordsworth expressed it in 'The Prelude':

There are in our existence spots of time,
That with distinct pre-eminence retain
A renovating virtue, whence – depressed
By false opinion and contentious thought,
Or aught of heavier or more deadly weight,
In trivial occupations, and the round
Of ordinary intercourse – our minds
Are nourished and invisibly repaired;
A virtue, by which pleasure is enhanced,
That penetrates, enables us to mount,
When high, more high, and lifts us up when fallen.[21]

Is what is being referred to here a moral or an aesthetic or a mystical experience? None of these categories is quite adequate, and the implied separation of our experience into such discrete components is in any case misleading. For in such moments of 'lifting up', referred to in many other passages in Wordsworth, and in the works of many other poetic and religious writers, there is a kind of integrated vision of the meaning of the whole. What 'lifts us up' is precisely the sense that our lives are not just a disorganized concatenation of contingent episodes, but that they are capable of fitting into a pattern of meaning, where responses of joy and thankfulness and compassion and love for our fellow creatures are intertwined, and where they make sense because they reflect a perfection and a richness that is not of our own making. Such a vision is patently at work in the

---

[21] William Wordsworth, 'The Prelude' Bk 12, 208–18 [1805 edition].

description of a transfigured reality set down by Thomas Traherne in the seventeenth century:

> The Corn was Orient and Immortal Wheat, which never should be reaped nor was ever sown. I thought it had stood from everlasting to everlasting. The Dust and Stones of the Street were as Precious as GOLD . . . And yong Men Glittering and Sparkling Angels, and Maids strange Seraphic Pieces of Life and Beauty! . . . Eternity was Manifest in the Light of the Day, and som thing infinit Behind evry thing appeared: which talked with my Expectation and moved my Desire.[22]

So stuck are many people with a reductive, naturalistic view of what constitutes 'reality' that, in spite of being moved by Traherne's lines, they may almost immediately step back and try to re-process them into a scientistic mould: there are the 'real' physical and chemical events (the photons bouncing off the cornfield and the cobblestones), and then there are some purely subjective occurrences in the mind of the poet. But why should any true scientist, or anyone who reflects on such passages in an open-minded way, try to force them into this rigid, two-piece naturalistic straitjacket? When Traherne sees the young people as 'strange Seraphic Pieces of Life and Beauty', he is seeing them 'transfigured' – that is, precisely *not* distorted by some subjective perceptual malfunction, but rather disclosed

---

[22] Thomas Traherne, 'The Third Century' [*c.* 1670], §3, in *Centuries, Poems and Thanksgivings*, Vol. 1, p. 111. Quoted in J. V. Taylor, *The Christlike God*, p. 33.

in their full meaning – in the richness and wonder and preciousness of their true humanity. What is disclosed is objective reality in all its meaning, just as, in the story of the Transfiguration, the disciples are able to see for the first time the true character of the teacher they followed, and the true meaning of his mission, into which they were now irreversibly caught up.

This seems to provide us with the right kind of model for understanding how divine interventions into the natural world might operate, if there are such things (and that possibility cannot be discounted, but neither can it be validated, by philosophy or science). They will not be marvels to gawp at, or demonstrations designed to coerce the sceptic, nor will they be ways of conferring beneficial outcomes on those who have been able to discover the trick of manipulating the divine will to further their chosen ends. There is the clearest indication in the Christian Gospels (in the story of Christ's decisive repudiation of such magical displays)[23] that this is not a morally or spiritually appropriate way to think of how God's power might properly be invoked in human affairs. Rather, they will be disclosures of meaning; that is, a lifting of the thin veil of mundanity that prevents us seeing the world in its true light. The events involved will be real, but 'real' does not imply reducibility to, on the one hand a demythologized natural component, and on the other hand a mere subjective occurrence in the mind of the beholder. Rather, if the picture presented here is

---

[23] In the narrative of the Temptation (Luke 4:1–13), Christ rejects the Devil's offer to turn stones into bread, or to enable him to fly, quoting Deuteronomy 6:16, 'Thou shalt not tempt the LORD thy God'.

anywhere near the mark, what will be brought about by the divine action, really and genuinely present in human history, is that the minds of the participants will, through grace, be 'nourished and invisibly repaired' so they can see the truth of what was really there all along.

Chapter 5

Belief and Meaning

And then I saw from that saying, 'He that cometh to me shall never hunger, and he that believeth on me shall never thirst' [John 6:35], that believing and coming was all one, and that he that came, that is, run out in his heart and affections after salvation by Christ, he indeed believed in Christ.

John Bunyan[1]

1. Truth and concealment

At the point we have now reached in our argument, it may be helpful to reflect a little more on the idea of 'disclosures of meaning' as the key to understanding some of the central miracles reported in the Christian Gospels. As underlined in the previous chapter, this does not involve denying the genuineness of divine intervention in the natural order, neither does it reduce such interventions merely to certain subjective responses or understandings in the minds of the beholder. What

---

[1] John Bunyan, *The Pilgrim's Progress* [1678], p. 143.

is claimed, rather, is that those who are enlightened by the transfiguring power of miraculous events are able to perceive something that was 'there all along' – something that was hidden, but is now disclosed. It is not a matter of in any way denying the reality and the truth of those events that are central to the faith; but it might involve giving up the conception of truth as something unambiguously 'bang in front of us' – present and open to the attentive scrutiny of any responsible observer.

To be sure, not even the crudest of empiricists expects every truth to be transparent to straightforward observation. There are many physical phenomena (for example at the micro level) that are hidden from ordinary view, and the existence and nature of which require highly sophisticated instruments and complex theoretical inferences to establish. What is more, as Einstein famously established, and as modern quantum theory also (for different reasons) insists, the position, speed, and indeed actions, of the observer may crucially interact with, and so affect, the reality that is observed. Nevertheless, when all these important qualifications are granted, the kind of truth investigated by the scientist remains, if I may so put it, *bald truth*: it is, so to speak, 'as it comes' – it is *there*, in a way that is entirely neutral with respect to what kind of agent (provided they possess the ordinary human intellectual and sensory capacities) is able to apprehend it. It presents itself to the subject, given that he or she is properly equipped with the right theories and methods and instruments, entirely without reference, for example, to their level of self-understanding, their moral development, or the stage they have reached in their individual spiritual journey through life. A cruel, a vicious, a bored, a venial, a corrupt, a hostile, a sceptical, an indifferent witness is just as equipped, scientifically speaking, to detect how this mixture in the test-tube reacts to the added catalyst – just as competent as the passionate, committed, devoted, responsible, deeply humane, morally sensitive observer. (The latter observer may of course be better *trusted*, to check the data accurately and write it up impartially, but that is quite another matter – it does not affect the 'bald' nature of the truths themselves.)

But there are many other kinds of truth that are clearly not 'bald' in this way. In the domain of literature, for example, the profound truths contained in the novels of Tolstoy, or the deep insights in the poetry of Shakespeare, may be entirely inaccessible to the bored or insensitive or corrupt reader. To be sure, the Bible, though it is in one way a literary text, is not regarded by the believer as an imaginative creation of the kind a novelist or poet might produce; certain specific historical claims are clearly involved. Yet despite that, we need to be on our guard to avoid the kind of distortion that can arise when our understanding of scriptural truth is assimilated to that of bald scientific truth; indeed, there is an increasing danger that what I have called 'bald' scientific truth is the *only* kind of truth our intellectual culture really acknowledges as genuine. Philosophers whose inquiries have traditionally ranged over a wide range of disciplines and modes of discourse might be expected to avoid this pitfall; but unfortunately philosophy itself has become increasingly attracted to a narrow scientistic model of truth and knowledge, and many of its most prominent current practitioners are less and less inclined to be open to more 'humane' modes of discourse – literary, poetic, aesthetic, religious – and are increasingly disposed to reduce the entire philosophical enterprise to a set of technical, quasi-scientific specialisms.[2]

To revert to the Gospel narratives, it is worth emphasizing that the 'mode of presentation' of many of the events recounted there is actually rather closer to that found in literary texts, as opposed to bald historical narratives. (One might add in passing that the boundary between history and literature is itself by no means as clear as those of a scientistic temperament might like to suppose, and it is doubtful whether there is even such a thing as a 'bald narrative' of events; but exploring this issue further at this point would take us too far afield.) In many of the key Gospel stories, although on the surface they take the form of plain, unadorned narrative, there is often a strange, luminous, paradoxical quality, a kind of 'aura of resonance'; and many elements of this aura are moral and spiritual in character, rather than being irreducible to a catalogue of raw observational data. Once this is grasped, it becomes clear why appreciating the truth of what happened will *not* be something available to each and every neutral observer. The events will be clear enough, but not in a 'bald' way; they will be objective, but their objective reality will be grasped not by everyone, only by those who have 'eyes to see' and 'ears to hear'. Just as much of the teaching of Jesus was in parables – so that their truth requires proper *discernment* rather than being presented 'bang in

2 See J. Cottingham, 'What is Humane Philosophy and Why is it at Risk?' [2009].

front of us' in an unequivocal way – so the various recorded events, if we look at them carefully, are very often more reminiscent of a text that has to be interpreted than an occurrence in a test-tube waiting to be checked and measured. The account of the feeding of the five thousand in Mark affords a good example of this. The Gospel writer does not (as one might expect from a modern advocate of the 'scientific' approach) rub in the massive empirical confirmation, or the unanimous testimony of the witnesses, but actually tells us that some of those closest to the events were unable to grasp them properly, or see their true significance: 'they did not understand about the loaves, for their hearts were hardened' (Mark 6:52). The reader of this, and of many other texts in all four Gospels, needs to go beyond a crude conception of truth as a straightforward observational match between a judgement and its object. What is needed is something closer to the idea explored by Martin Heidegger, when he drew upon the Greek conception of truth as *alêtheia* (literally 'unconcealing'): truth involves an *uncovering*, a bringing something out of concealment.[3]

Defenders of a certain kind of religious fundamentalism sometimes endeavour to claim the 'high ground' with respect to truth, suggesting that anything short of an absolutely plain, 'no-nonsense' interpretation of the events such as the Resurrection is a fudge. They implicitly advocate what one might call a 'video camera' account of the relevant events: if we imagine that a camcorder had been placed outside the tomb early on the morning of 7 April in the year AD 30 (if that is the correct

---

[3] Martin Heidegger, *Being and Time* [1927], §219.

historical date for the Sunday immediately following the Roman execution of Jesus of Nazareth in Jerusalem), and if we suppose that the instrument had somehow been sealed in a time capsule and preserved for inspection today, then the image on the hard disk would show the stone at the mouth of the tomb suddenly rolling aside, the risen Christ issuing forth, the angels entering the tomb, folding the grave-clothes and awaiting the arrival of the disciples, and so on . . . The event, in short, is to be understood in terms of the 'bald' scientific model of truth discussed above: it is supposed to be susceptible in principle to exactly the same *kind* of experiential confirmation as might be available for any other historical event (such as, for example, the eruption of Mount Vesuvius in AD 79). Is this how the defender of the truth of the Resurrection has to proceed? The strategy has its attractions: it has a certain robustness about it that arguably has more integrity than the 'liberal' theological line which relies on treating the whole story as some kind of myth or subsequent embellishment. Nevertheless, in the next section, we shall begin to unravel some of the ways in which this seemingly cut-and-dried approach risks going astray.

2. Evidence and accessibility

For a believer to wish to invoke the strength of scientific evidence in order to establish the truth of a religious worldview is understandable enough, and our contemporary culture puts such a premium on the bald scientific model of truth that departing from it can seem like abandoning any claim to truth whatsoever. Nevertheless, there are many reasons for being wary of such an approach. The philosopher Ludwig Wittgenstein, who spent much time wrestling with questions of religious belief, was adamant in rejecting the idea that something like the Resurrection could be established or refuted by appeal to a 'historic[al] basis in the sense that the ordinary belief in historic[al] facts could serve as a foundation'.[4] I take Wittgenstein's underlying point here to be that the role of evidence in religious commitment is entirely different from that which it occupies on the 'Humean' model – a dispassionate scrutiny of empirical probabilities based on past instances.[5] The kind of evidence which, for the believer, supports faith is not evidence assessed from a detached standpoint, but experience that is available only as a result of certain inner transformations. Saying this does *not* imply some kind of subjectivism about religious truth; it merely makes the point that there may be some truths the *accessibility conditions* of which include certain requirements as to the attitude of the subject.[6]

To introduce the idea of a special kind of evidence requiring the need for 'inner transformation' may look to some people like a fallback position – a hastily devised escape route for the beleaguered modern theist who has been forced by Humean and other Enlightenment critics of religion to abandon the

---

4 Based on notes taken by Wittgenstein's students, *c*. 1938; in *Lectures and Conversations on Aesthetics, Psychology and Religious Belief*, p. 57.

5 David Hume, *An Enquiry Concerning Human Understanding* [1748], Section X.

6 For more on the idea of 'accessibility conditions', see Cottingham, 'What Difference Does It Make?' [2006]. Compare also Cottingham, *The Spiritual Dimension* [2005], Ch. 5.

straightforward factualism about, for example, the Resurrection that characterized the simpler, if more naïve, devout faith of the past. In a stimulating recent study, however, the theologian Sarah Coakley has convincingly shown that even if we go back to earliest times, to the New Testament narratives, we find the need for inner 'epistemic transformation' presented as a prerequisite for witnessing the Resurrection. Thus the story in Matthew does not (as a modern spin doctor might perhaps do) enhance the dossier with overwhelming 'objective' evidence, but adds the telling phrase 'but some doubted', *even in the very sentence* that reports the Galilee appearance of the risen Christ (Matthew 28:17). Or again, the narrative in John of the appearance in the locked room on the Sunday after Easter suggests that 'some change in one's normal demands for perceptual evidences' were needed to recognize the risen body (John 20:24–28). And the Emmaus story in Luke implies that 'a narrowly noetic [intellectual] investigation would take one *nowhere* in this quest', and that 'evidences of the heart . . . could not be neglected if Christ-as-risen were to be apprehended' (Luke 24:28–35).[7]

The idea of 'evidences of the heart', reminiscent of Pascal,[8] is in line with a fair amount of recent philosophical work on the emotions by a number of authors, which has begun to explore

---

[7] Sarah Coakley, *Powers and Submissions* [2002], p. 140. Coakley's discussion includes an insightful chapter on 'Wittgenstein and Resurrection Epistemology' to which I am indebted here.

[8] Blaise Pascal, *Pensées* [*c.* 1660], ed. Lafuma, No. 424: *C'est le coeur qui sent Dieu et non la raison. Voilà ce que c'est que la foi* ('It's the heart, not Reason, that senses God: that is what faith is').

the idea that emotional responses are not merely an extraneous affective addition to the factual or propositional content of a belief, but involve transformative ways of perceiving reality – ways of uncovering patterns of salience that were previously hidden. The Emmaus narrative is particularly significant in this context. Luke's description is at pains to emphasize the sequence of emotional responses in the protagonists – to begin with, the sullen silence when they first encounter the stranger and he asks them what events they are discussing: 'they stopped in their tracks, sullen faced' (*estathêsan skuthrôpoi*, 24:17); next, the 'burning' of the hearts as he expounds the scriptures to them (cf. 24:32); then the warm impulse of offering hospitality to the stranger ('stay with us, for the day is far spent', 24:29); and finally the 'opening of the eyes' at the breaking of the bread (24:31). All this depends on an intricate interplay involving affective and cognitive aspects of the perceptions of those involved. The failure of the travellers to recognize the risen Christ when he first joined them on the road was not just a cognitive one, a matter of their being *anoêtoi* (foolish), but was also a function of their being 'slow of *heart*' (*bradeis tê kardia*, 24:25).

Some may object to invoking the role of the emotions in this way, on the grounds that it leads us, once more, into the danger of a 'subjectivizing' interpretation of central religious doctrines such as that of the Resurrection. When St Paul said, 'if Christ was not raised from the dead, our faith is in vain and we are lying witnesses',[9] was he not presupposing the straightforward

---

[9] 1 Corinthians 15:14–15.

factual truth of the Resurrection as a simple historical event that, by implication, could have been witnessed by anyone, however detached and sceptical, who was there at the time? By contrast, does not Coakley's talk of the 'epistemic transformation' needed if the risen Christ was to be apprehended come suspiciously close to saying it was not a fact at all, in the normal scientific or historical sense of 'fact' – something objectively detectable by any physiologically normal observer – but was merely a kind of subjective illusion, capable of being experienced only by someone in some kind of emotionally disturbed or hyped-up condition?

These alleged implications do not follow. First, from a theological point of view, stressing the need for emotional transformation in the subject does not rule out the possibility of genuine divine agency, nor is it incompatible with a genuine external and objective causation of such transformation. Second, on a philosophical level, one may cite many cases of perfectly genuine and objective facts which nevertheless can only be detected by those who are, in virtue of internal transformations, in an epistemically privileged position. One paradigm instance of this is in the domain of music, where there may be complex objective properties of a musical work which simply cannot be apprehended by 'any physiologically normal observer', but which require perhaps long years of habituation and training, and sharpening of emotional and aesthetic sensibility, in order to be detected. Many other examples could be cited from other fields. In short, the notion of 'privileged receptivity', as it may be termed, is an epistemically respectable notion with a wide application, and one which the religious apologist may therefore invoke without risk of being accused either of special pleading, or of subjectivizing the facts in question. To say the emotions can open our eyes is not at all to say that what we see is merely the creature of our emotions. Just as emotion can distort (for example, infatuation can blind one to someone's moral defects), so it can illuminate (as when affection enables one to discern genuine sterling qualities of character in a friend which the casual acquaintance may have missed).

3. Vision and transformation

So where does this leave us when it comes to the question of the foundational events of Christianity? Believers will want to say that the relevant events were real, and that they were really witnessed by the disciples. None of this has been denied in the above discussion. But what has been added is that what counts as reality should not be understood exclusively on a scientific model, as something that is available for inspection or testing by any dispassionate observer, irrespective of, for example, their character, receptivity or moral insight.

It is worth adding here that the very notion of a 'scientific model' of reality is itself somewhat problematic. This may be seen if we reflect a little about the standard criteria for someone's perceiving or verifying something. Many philosophers (though few would nowadays call themselves positivists) are still surprisingly influenced by the kind of atomistic template offered by empiricists such as David Hume, where a given proposition is supposed to be taken on its own, checked against one or more sensory impressions, and pronounced true or false. Did the substance in the test-tube turn green? We appear to be able to pronounce on the truth or otherwise of this claim almost in complete isolation from anything else. And perhaps this inclines us to think that 'Did Christ rise from the dead?' can be answered in the 'video-camera' mode, as a simple function of whether a small set of detached and impersonal scientific observations about a re-animated corpse could or could not have been made on the first Easter morning.

Yet much philosophy of knowledge in the last half-century or more has persuasively argued that we should abandon the idea that there are straightforwardly verifiable 'basic propositions' the truth of which is just 'given' in observation. At first it seems simple enough: when I see the red apple, there is an experiential datum – a 'given' – and it is this that confers authority on my statement 'This is red.' But such a notion – the 'myth of the given', as the influential American philosopher Wilfred Sellars calls it – turns out in the end to be highly dubious. For the correctness of my judgement about this apple's being red actually depends on a whole network of complex linguistic conventions about the standard conditions for the appropriate use of the predicate 'red' (roughly, something counts as red only if it would be called 'red' by a normal English-speaking observer in normal light). So the picture of what is 'given' somehow validating my knowledge *in isolation* must be wrong. Such epistemic atomism needs to give way to a much more holistic conception of perceptual knowledge. It is, Sellars argues, 'a matter of simple logic, that one couldn't have observational knowledge of *any* fact unless one knew many *other* things as well'.[10]

If the atomistic model fails even for very simple examples of ordinary perception of a single object ('This is a red apple'), it becomes vastly more inadequate when we are dealing with events that are pregnant with deep moral and spiritual significance. As our earlier discussion of the Emmaus narrative in Luke shows, the description of what the disciples saw and heard that day is *not* best understood as recording a set of simple observational confirmations of a set of plain empirical facts, but rather as narrating a complex learning sequence, where the protagonists were led to recognize the risen Christ in the light of a new, enriched awareness they had been helped to achieve about the meaning of his life and his continued presence with them. The text itself invites us to construe the dramatic experience of the disciples as a matter of discernment or *hermeneusis* rather than of simple empirical verification: their hearts and minds were opened so that they could *understand and interpret* what had happened to them. Endlessly repeated scratchings at the question, 'Did the Resurrection or did it not *really happen?*' paradoxically manage to take our attention away from something crucial about the Emmaus account as we have it: namely that the story involves a change, a moral and spiritual transformation in the lives of the disciples – a shift from sullenness, anxiety and despair to joyful excitement and hope.

---

10 Wilfred Sellars, 'The Myth of the Given' [1956].

Without that necessary element, without the protagonists and those who came after them grasping the deeper significance of what had happened, the whole event would have been pointless – for what could possibly be of human value and meaning simply in the mere biological demonstration that a previously dead person could be resuscitated and seen to be alive for a few weeks? Those zealous for the faith might wish, no doubt for the best of motives, to rewrite the Gospels so that they provide 'cast-iron evidence'; they might wish to reshape the accounts of the Resurrection so that they describe a number of scientifically certified episodes which constrain the assent even of the most sceptical. But what, in the end, would be the point of that? What conceivable salvific gain would there be in the lives of these new 'believers' – how could such certified paranormal displays be construed as advancing in the slightest Christ's divine mission to seek out and save lost humanity, to call his followers to repentance and to a new life of love and self-sacrifice? As soon as this question is asked, it should become clear that in this sort of context religious faith loses its very *raison d'être* unless it is bound up in the closest possible way with the moral and spiritual transformation of the believer.

4. Moral growth and spiritual conversion

At this point, it may be helpful to return to Pascal's idea of the 'reasons of the heart' and make a connection with Heidegger's idea of truth as an 'unconcealment', or disclosing, referred to in the first section of this chapter. Part of the importance of the emotions in human life, as hinted at by the account of how the disciples' hearts 'burned within them' on the road to Emmaus, is that they can have an 'unblocking' function, allowing us to understand ourselves and the world better, by revealing and bringing to the surface what we had previously concealed from ourselves, or been blocked from perceiving properly. Often such outflowings of emotion are the trigger for moral and spiritual change: the scales fall from someone's eyes, and they are brought to see that some present course of action, or even their life as a whole, needs to change.

An example from literature may (as is often the case) help to make vivid, in imaginative terms, a phenomenon that will be familiar enough to many people from their own experience. Looking at the crisis that has overwhelmed him, Thomas Wolsey, in Shakespeare's *Henry VIII*, declares in his misery that he 'feels his heart new open'd'.

> I have ventured,
> Like little wanton boys that swim on bladders,
> This many summers in a sea of glory,
> But far beyond my depth: my high-blown pride
> At length broke under me and now has left me,
> Weary and old with service, to the mercy
> Of a rude stream, that must for ever hide me.
> Vain pomp and glory of this world, I hate ye:
> I feel my heart new open'd.[11]

---

[11] W. Shakespeare, *A History of Henry VIII* [1613], Act III, scene 2.

Things suddenly look different, and the 'high blown pride' that has motivated Wolsey for most of his career is now seen as having carried him 'far beyond his depth', into vanities that now for the first time seem to him hateful. The example is not an explicitly religious one, nor is it described by Shakespeare in religious terms. But it would be a mistake to make a watertight separation between episodes of moral growth and change and the kind of spiritual awakening that is described, for example, in the Emmaus narrative, and in many other biblical stories.

What is common to such episodes is the sense of a turning point, a change often marked for the protagonists by intense psychological turmoil. In the strange yet highly suggestive story of Balaam in the Hebrew Bible, the prophet is in a state of fury and frustration as he tries to force his unwilling donkey along a certain path. Only when the animal takes on human speech and rebukes him for his cruelty are his eyes opened, so that he can now see the angel of the Lord standing in the path and barring the way.[12] His whole view of the journey on which he is embarked needs to change.

Quite apart from the fact that such biblical examples involve alleged supernatural intervention (which may lead to such episodes being dismissed out of hand by the sceptic), some readers may be inclined to wonder whether the general view of moral change presented here may not be somewhat hyperbolical: is not the reality a good deal more prosaic and straightforward? Typical moral development (our imaginary critic may object) takes place in human society when an individual is

---

12 Numbers 22:22–28.

inducted as a child into a certain ethical culture.[13] As a result of training from parents and teachers, which begins at a very early age, the infant is encouraged to develop certain feelings and attitudes, such as truthfulness, respect for others and so on. Initially, this is not much more than a conditioning process: when the emotional and behaviour responses are 'good', they will be rewarded with praise and approval, and when they are 'bad', they will be discouraged with disapproval and perhaps punishment. The inverted commas around 'good' and 'bad' signal the fact that at this stage the child need have no clear rational grasp of exactly what makes the relevant actions good or bad; she is simply being habituated to identify certain classes of action with those that elicit favourable or unfavourable responses from adults. But soon there will be a transitional stage, when the child begins to discern the rationale for this approval and disapproval. And finally, as the child comes of age, she should reach the stage of fully internalizing the relevant encouragements and prohibitions, not just in a mechanical or conditioned way, but with an appreciation of what it is about the conduct in question that makes it praiseworthy or blameworthy. The outcome of this gradual process, if all goes well, is a person of mature ethical virtue: someone who has the right habits of feeling and action, but who also has the capacity to discern what should be done, and why – someone who acts, as Aristotle puts it, 'knowing what he is doing and choosing it for its own sake', and who has the right feelings 'at the right times

---

13 For an insightful development of this theme, see Sabina Lovibond, *Ethical Formation* [2002].

on the right grounds towards the right people, for the right motive and in the right way'.[14]

The calm Aristotelian ideal just sketched takes us worlds away from the notion of individual life as structured by moments of moral and spiritual crisis. It envisages, instead, members of moral communities who are lucky enough to be 'at home' in the ethical climate they inhabit, so that their perception of what is right accords with their spontaneous emotional responses. Such fortunate individuals achieve a genuine moral equilibrium in their lives. First, they wholly escape the pitfalls of bad character – the degraded condition of deliberately pursuing what is wrong. Second, they manage to avoid the backsliding that is characteristic of those who might like to pursue the good but lapse through weakness – as St Paul painfully put it, 'the good that I would, that I do not, and the evil that I would not, that I do'.[15] Third, they achieve a more harmonious life even than those who manage to act rightly, but only because they have the self-control to prevent themselves falling into temptation. Rising above all these less desirable states, the ethically fortunate denizens of Aristotle's world lead balanced lives of true, unfettered virtue: their desires, inclinations, goals and actions all dovetail harmoniously with what is rational and right.[16] This may be a rosy picture of successful induction into a life of full ethical virtue, but (given the right

---

[14] Aristotle, *Nicomachean Ethics* [*c.* 325 BC], Bk II, Ch. 4 and Ch. 6, 1105a31–2 and 1106b21–2.

[15] Romans 7:19.

[16] For these four grades of conduct and outlook in Aristotelian ethics, see J. Cottingham, *Philosophy and the Good Life* [1998], Ch. 2.

innate dispositions, the right upbringing and the right oppor-
tunities for developing the appropriate sensibilities) many
readers may feel that it ought to be well within the bounds of
human possibility.

The message from the Judaeo-Christian tradition is that
things are very seldom as simple as the secular Aristotelian
model envisages.[17] Christian and Judaic views about the inher-
ently flawed character of humankind, dramatized as the doctrine of the Fall, imply that the path of righteousness is never
an easy one. There may be a dispute here between those who
might side with Aristotle in constructing a fairly optimistic
map of the conditions for the good life, and those who might
be drawn to a gloomier assessment of the inherent sinfulness of
humankind. That debate, between what might broadly be
called the Pelagian and the Augustinian perspectives,[18] has of
course conditioned much of the history of Western religious
and ethical thought. But rather than broaching that vast debate
in its generality, I want to focus on one particular strand in
Christian thought, the idea of *conversion*, or *metanoia*, which
seems particularly relevant to understanding the role of the
emotions in ethical and spiritual development, and also to

---

[17] In what follows, I shall confine myself to the Christian case, but it seems
probable that there are similar points to be made about the other two great
Abrahamic faiths, not to mention other major world religions including
Buddhism.

[18] Pelagius (fifth century) asserted the perfectability of humankind, and his
views were the subject of a series of attacks by Augustine (such as *On Nature
and Grace* [415]), which firmly established the doctrine of original sin
as essential to Christianity.

explicating the associated idea that eyes can thereby be opened, and reality disclosed in its true meaning.

The Greek term *metanoia* is a complex one. In Classical Greek, for example in Thucydides, it refers simply to an afterthought, a change of mind; though even here there is the idea of an emotional shift. The Athenians, after the revolt of Mytilene, were initially minded to put to death the entire male population and enslave the women and children. But 'next day', Thucydides relates, 'there was a sudden change of feeling (*metanoia*), and people began to think how cruel and how unprecedented such a decision was – to destroy not only the guilty but the entire population of a state'.[19] (This more merciful view eventually prevailed.) In the Christian Gospels, the term *metanoia* takes on the idea of a radical revision or fundamental reorientation of outlook: the call, first of John the Baptist, then of Jesus of Nazareth, was a call to 'Repent (*metanoieite*), for the kingdom of heaven is at hand!' (Matthew 3:2 and 4:17). This is not just a request to change one's mind about certain previous decisions, but a demand for a complete change of life. The striking image used in the fourth Gospel is one of being re-born (John 3:1–7).

What are the conditions for such a radical shift of outlook? By using the term 'conditions', I am not asking about logically or causally necessary conditions. In the domain of moral and psychological growth, we should not, as Aristotle famously said of ethics in general, require more precision than the subject-

---

[19] Thucydides, *History of the Peloponnesian War* [*c.* 415 BC], Bk III, §36; trans. R. Warner, p. 180.

matter admits of,[20] and it seems extremely unlikely that one could specify some universal *sine qua non* for such changes. Nor am I asking about sufficient conditions, since a total specification of these (even leaving aside the question of supernatural or divine action) would probably have to include all kinds of social, psychological and physiological factors which even to attempt to list would be a tedious and perhaps unending task. Instead, I shall confine myself to the far more modest task of suggesting what might be called *facilitating conditions* – that is to say, conditions which we have good reason to suppose play a crucial role in at least some central cases of conversion or change of outlook.

The conversion of Saul of Tarsus provides one such case; and it is of interest that it was a change abrupt and radical enough to be flagged – by his assumption of a new name – as a complete personal and moral rebirth. There is a paradox about Paul, in that he spent a great deal of his subsequent energies as a Christian engaging in intricate intellectual and scriptural debate with those he was trying to convert. But his own conversion, from the little we know about it, was certainly not the outcome of rational discussion, but was a sudden, emotionally shattering episode marked by a serious collapse: he fell down, and was, for several days, unable to see (Acts 9:1–9). What can have precipitated this? The theological answer is, of course, clear: it was the voice of the risen Christ, who spoke to him out of a bright light. But the record also contains a vital clue to the 'facilitating conditions', namely the fact that earlier in his life

---

[20] *Nicomachean Ethics*, Bk I, Ch. 3.

Saul had been present, not as an instigator, but as an apparently willing young supporter (holding the coats of the executioners), at the stoning of the martyr Stephen (Acts 6:8–15, and 7:54—8:1). He went on from this to a career as a zealous persecutor of the Christians; but the account of the stoning provided in Acts leaves no doubt that the episode must have been one likely to call forth the horror and pity of any morally decent person. One does not have to indulge in too much amateur psychoanalysis to conjecture that the internal tensions generated in the young man by having to repress these feelings built up to the point where only something like a nervous breakdown could release the moral energies which would set him on a new course.

It is important, once again, to warn that pointing to such elements in the story should not necessarily be taken as offering a reductionist and 'psychologizing' account of the events described. For the kinds of reason already underlined several times in our previous discussions, believers will want to be very wary of subjectivizing interpretations; but they should also be wary of going too far in the opposite direction, towards a bald fundamentalism. To insist that the conversion of Paul was *entirely* a function of a spectacular divine action in the form of an empirically verifiable blinding light would not only falsify the text (the light apparently did not affect Paul's companions) but would involve a theologically repugnant idea of God as one who compels human allegiance by irresistible supernatural intervention. Such a conception of the deity is morally and theologically dubious, because it is incompatible with the idea that God always allows space for free human choice in accepting or rejecting his call. As Pascal luminously observes:

> Our religion asserts . . . that God . . . has hidden himself from direct human knowledge; indeed, the very name he gives himself in Scripture is *Deus absconditus* – the hidden God [Isaiah 45:15] . . . God has appointed visible signs . . . to make himself known to those who seek him sincerely; and . . . he has nonetheless veiled these signs in such a way that he will be discerned only by those who seek him with all their heart.[21]

The 'signs' Pascal is referring to here are the Christian sacraments, but, as our previous discussion of the Resurrection indicates, the point may be generalized to cover other instances of divine self-manifestation. Christ himself is reported to have said that only an 'evil and adulterous generation looks for a sign' (Matthew 16:4). The theological point, I take it, is that God does not constrain or manipulate allegiance by paranormal demonstrations; the ethical point is that following the path of righteousness is something that must be freely chosen without the kind of dubious motivational impulse that any unequivocal display of divine power would produce. A God who leaves space for his creatures to accept or reject him must intervene only in a way that respects that freedom. The entire biblical tradition portrays God as seeking a response from his creatures, but it is a *response*, not a constrained reaction: it emerges and grows out of

---

21 Pascal, *Pensées* [*c.* 1660], ed. Lafuma, No. 427.

a change in the inner life of the subject, rather than being an effect of 'shock and awe' (in the American military sense).

Paul was not compelled by main force to believe in the risen Christ; but he was called to acknowledge it, in a manner that went against the grain of his entire previous career as a zealous Pharisee. If we are to explain this in a way that does not represent the new, converted Paul as a puppet or a zombie, then we are surely required to suppose that the change he underwent involved the awakening of something in him that had previously been buried or repressed. Rational argument and scientific evidence alone could not have achieved the change; neither could 'religious experience' – if that simply means more 'evidence' in the form of visions of supernatural forces – have succeeded in producing the change, or at least the right *type* of change. What was needed was the 'reasons of the heart': the kind of deep emotional response at a pre-rational level that allowed his angry, aggressive, persecutory ego to begin to fall away, and the healing process to begin, which would release his true self, the self he was called to be.

The account of Paul's conversion tells us that it took several days for him to recover his sight. It does not need an expert in human psychology to point out that the process of healing in such cases can often be a long and perilous one, and indeed the idea of a radical rupture in previous patterns of thought and feeling is clearly one that presents many risks. Yet as the poet Hölderlin observes, 'Where danger lies, the saving power grows strong': *Wo aber Gefahr ist, wächst Das Rettende auch.*[22] The

---

[22] Friedrich Hölderlin, 'Patmos' [1806].

complexity and the difficulty of the process of internal spiritual transformation should not make us shy away from it, or marginalize its importance in a meaningful human life. In one of his later essays, Carl Jung wrote that the churches were too concerned with bolstering themselves as mass movements, and insufficiently attentive to 'their real task of helping the individual achieve a *metanoia* – a rebirth of the Spirit, *Deo concedente* [if God so grants]'.[23] One does not need to suggest that all religious conversion is the psychologically complex process referred to by Jung or suggested in the above discussion of the Pauline example. Conversion can no doubt take many forms, sometimes rapid, sometimes protracted – as Gerard Manley Hopkins puts it, either 'at once, as once at a crash Paul', or else 'as Austin [Augustine], lingering-out sweet skill ...'.[24] The latter image is of a protracted philosophical wrestling – though even in this Augustinian case it was clearly not just an intellectual matter, but involved a complex interior descent, a journey to the depths of the psyche.[25] At all events, what our discussion so far suggests is that conversion will always involve a characteristic emotional shift, allowing the world to be seen differently, and allowing a reality hitherto concealed to be disclosed in its true meaning.

To set against the relatively calm and ordered process of ethical development envisaged in classical Aristotelian virtue

---

[23] C. G. Jung, 'The Undiscovered Self' [1957], in *Collected Works*, Vol. 10, §§488–588; repr. in A. Storr (ed.), *Jung, Selected Writings*, p. 376.

[24] Gerard Manley Hopkins, 'The Wreck of the Deutschland', stanza 10; in *Poems (1876–1889)*.

[25] 'Go not outside, but return within thyself; in the inward man dwelleth the truth.' *De vera religione* [AD 391], xxxix, 72.

theory, the religious idea of conversion takes seriously both our 'wretchedness' and our 'redeemability' – the two poles of the human condition described by Pascal.[26] True moral and spiritual growth, on this picture, requires us to be shaken out of our ordinary complacency; it requires us to bring to the surface those 'reasons of the heart' which will open us to new ways of perceiving, and new possibilities for enriched awareness. Conversion, if this is right, is not a coercive process engineered by demonstrations of power, but is a response of the whole person – intellectual, emotional, moral, spiritual – that enables what was hitherto hidden to come to light. The process is not one of being brought up short by new scientific evidence or paranormal events, but the working of an interior change that generates a new openness. Nothing can force acceptance unless we have 'ears to hear'.[27] And what is heard is not a barrage of confirmatory data, but a message that needs to be understood. It is, as the second epistle of Peter beautifully puts it, a *word* – one that must be 'heeded, as a light that shines in a dark place, until the day dawns and the morning star rises in your hearts'.[28]

---

[26] 'Christian faith serves to establish virtually only two things: the corruption of our nature, and our redemption through Jesus Christ'. *Pensées*, ed. Lafuma, No. 427. Compare No 6: 'the wretchedness of man without God; the felicity of man with God'.

[27] Matthew 11:15; Mark 4:9.

[28] 2 Peter 1:19.

Chapter 6

Learning to Believe

Life can educate you to a belief in God.

Ludwig Wittgenstein[1]

1. The lessons of life

If our line of thought in the previous two chapters has been right, something will have emerged about the kind of change required for religious conversion – the kind of change that marks the shift from being a sceptic or an agnostic to becoming a believer. In discussing the accounts that have come down to us of the foundational event of Christianity, the Resurrection of Christ, I have drawn attention to the fact that the shift of perspective undergone by the earlier disciples was evidently not simply a cognitive one, not simply the amassing of a body of empirical evidence; as the records make abundantly clear, it involved an emotional change that allowed them to see things in a new way.

Ludwig Wittgenstein once observed that 'a religious belief could only be (something like) passionately committing

---

[1] From a manuscript of 1950, in L. Wittgenstein, *Culture and Value*, p. 97.

oneself to a system of reference.'[2] In line with this, we may say that the early disciples seized passionately upon a new framework of interpretation: what had seemed the total failure of a horrible and humiliating execution was now perceived as the prelude to the triumphant proclamation of a message of hope. But recognizing the 'passionate' element should not lead us to construe this interpretive shift as *merely* an emotional matter – simply a matter of feelings, without any cognitive change or shift in belief contents.[3] This would surely be an implausible view, since the early disciples, and subsequent Christians, in adopting such a framework, surely *did* shift their beliefs: with the new framework went not just a return from despair to faith in God, but an accompanying belief that his power had indeed been manifested in the presence to them of the risen Christ.

Some may think this kind of shift is much harder for us, in the more sceptical climate of today, than it was in the world of the first century AD. Many indeed may feel a strong affinity with Wittgenstein's own personal position when he contemplated the possibility of conversion: he felt unable to embrace the Christian framework, since, as he observed, he could not bring himself to make the belief shift.[4] *But he did believe the belief shift could occur.* This is clearly shown by one of his most pregnant remarks, which provides the epigraph for the present chapter: 'Life can educate you to a belief in God.'

---

[2] Wittgenstein, *Culture and Value*, p. 73.

[3] See J. Cottingham, 'The Lessons of Life' [2009].

[4] Wittgenstein, manuscript of 1937, in *Culture and Value*, p. 37.

There is a powerful fictional example in Tolstoy's novel *Anna Karenina* which illuminates in vivid imaginative terms something of the real-life phenomenon to which Wittgenstein pointed. In the second half of the book, we see the hero of the novel, Konstantin Levin, enjoying a relatively successful and secure marriage – one portrayed by Tolstoy as a counterpart to the ill-fated marriage of the eponymous heroine. At the relevant point in the story, Levin has been waiting for his pregnant wife Kitty, who is long overdue, to give birth. After a troubled night, punctuated with a protracted argument triggered by his wife's distress at his having come home very late after an evening drinking at his club, followed by a visit with friends to the house of the captivating but emotionally disturbed Anna, the labour suddenly begins. Levin is at once in torment:

> 'Kostya, please don't be frightened, it's nothing. I'm not afraid at all,' she said, seeing his frightened face, and she pressed his hand to her breast, then to her lips. Levin was still struck by what was uncovered to him now, when all the veils were suddenly taken away and the very core of her soul shone in her eyes. And in that simplicity and nakedness she, the very one he loved, was still more visible. She looked at him and smiled, but suddenly her eyebrows twitched, she raised her head, and quickly going up to him, took his hand and pressed all of herself to him, so that he could feel her hot breath on him. She was suffering and seemed to be complaining to him of her suffering . . .
>
> 'Lord, have mercy, forgive us, help us!', Levin repeated

words that somehow suddenly came to his lips. And he, an unbeliever, repeated these words not just with his lips. Now, in that moment, he knew that neither all his doubts nor the impossibility he knew in himself of believing by means of reason, hindered him in the least from addressing God. It all blew off his soul like dust. To whom was he to turn if not to Him in whose hands he felt himself, his soul and his love to be?[5]

All sorts of dismissive interpretations of this passage may occur to the sceptical mind. Perhaps Levin is so beside himself with anxiety that he goes against his better judgement and indulges in a superstitious ritual that he rationally knows can do no good. But that deflationary reading will not survive serious scrutiny of the text and its full context. Levin has always loved Kitty, but previously in a fierce, possessive and somewhat controlling way that made him genuinely miserable when (earlier in the novel) he thought his suit would not be successful. At the start of the crucial episode of her confinement he has lapsed into a sort of complacency: the earlier torments of courtship are over, and Kitty is now his devoted wife, happily involved in her domestic pursuits and preparation for impending motherhood. But now Levin's perceptions undergo a radical shift. As the pangs of labour begin to shake her, and he is confronted with the mysterious process of childbirth, and the very real danger that process poses to her own life, he sees for the first

---

[5]   Leo Tolstoy, *Anna Karenina* [1873–7], Part VII, Ch. 13.

time her true beauty and integrity. In that moment, his heart is opened to the mystery and fragility and wonder and terror of life and of love, and he begins to pray. His decision could never have been arrived at by cold scrutiny of the evidence; indeed, Levin knows in himself the 'impossibility in himself of believing by means of reason'. But only a religious framework is now adequate for interpreting the momentous truths to which his heart has now been opened. He prays to God, and repeats the words 'not just with his lips'. He believes.

It is important to underline that what Levin undergoes is not a 'religious experience' in the sense of a vision of angels or other supernatural influences, but rather a certain opening of the heart, and an associated heightening of moral awareness. Tolstoy, with great delicacy and a keen insight into the nature of the religious journey, resists the temptation to present the reader with a neat 'once for all' moment of change. Further anxieties, further intellectual agonizings, and further deepenings of moral and emotional awareness, are needed in order to consolidate Levin's new-found faith. Although doubts still occur, Levin is eventually able to dismiss them as dishonest – as a kind of lack of integrity or bad faith: 'He could not admit that he had known the truth then and was now mistaken ... because he cherished his state of soul of that time, and by admitting that it had been due to weakness he would have profaned those moments.'[6] At the close of the novel he is able to declare to himself: 'This new feeling hasn't changed me, hasn't made me happy or suddenly enlightened, as I dreamed – just like the

---

6 Tolstoy, *Anna Karenina*, p. 787; from Part VIII, Ch. 9.

feeling for my son. Nor was there any surprise. And faith or not faith – I don't know what it is – but this feeling has entered into me just as imperceptibly through suffering and has firmly lodged itself in my soul.'[7] Life has educated him to a belief in God.

The moral, perhaps, for all those (including philosophers) who have agonized over the 'the great cry of "I would like to believe but unfortunately I cannot"'[8] is that their problem can never be resolved by intellectual inquiry alone. Konstantin Levin was able to make the religious commitment, with its associated belief shift, partly because he had been inducted as a child into forms of religious praxis which had made the framework he embraced accessible to him, and given it shape and significance. The other catalyst for his conversion, also a form of education, was the 'education' provided by life – the actual structure of the perception-changing experiences he underwent during his wife's confinement and in the phase of his life that followed it. It should be no surprise that an emotional, moral and spiritual shift can accomplish what merely intellectual theorizing is powerless to do. So many of the significant changes in our lives are like that: reason, intellect, may be a crucial part of who we are, but in such cases it often limps along behind. Before we can see, before we can believe, the interior response has to occur. In a way that is in some ways analogous to what happens in the psychotherapeutic context, it is the lowering of the hard defences of the controlling intellect

---

[7] *Anna Karenina*, p. 817; from Part VIII Ch. 19.
[8] See Richard Swinburne, *Faith and Reason* [2nd edn, 2003], Ch 3.

that allows growth and healing.[9] Wittgenstein, who never himself managed to make the crucial shift, nevertheless perhaps glimpsed this important truth, in a comment from a manuscript of 1937: 'The *edifice of your pride has* to be dismantled. And that means frightful work'.[10]

2. Prevailing images of belief: exclusivism

Those who have made the shift to religious belief, those who still hold back, and indeed those who are not at all drawn in that direction, may all in different ways and for different reasons be interested in the question of what difference religious belief makes to the life of the believer. Forming a clear view of this is made harder by a whole series of prejudices regarding the nature of the religious outlook; so it may be useful at this point to list three of the most persistent and in each case add some comments which may serve to untangle some of the misconceptions. All the instances I shall mention have at least a grain of truth about them, and there are certainly many believers who have in the past, or do now, hold views of the kind mentioned. In that sense, they provide not entirely unfair ammunition for the increasingly militant secularism of our times. But I shall suggest that in each case the attitudes in question need to be understood properly. In the form in which they are often presented by critics, they are aberrations rather than

---

9 See J. Cottingham, *Philosophy and the Good Life*, Ch. 4.
10 'Das *Gebäude Deines Stolzes* ist abzutragen. Und das gibt furchtbare Arbeit', in *Culture and Value*, p. 30.

essential aspects of religious faith; we need to discard the specious husk and uncover the authentic core.

Let us begin by focusing on the charge of *exclusivism* – a notion which many see as inseparable from the typical religious outlook. The charge may crudely but aptly be expressed as follows:

> *(A) 'Religious believers think they have an exclusive passport to heaven.'*

Well, no doubt some believers do think this. But, as some of our previous discussions should have made clear, religious allegiance is not properly understood as some magical key to success, either in this world or the next. Such a crude conception could only work for those who compartmentalize – who think that you can isolate a credal package, allegiance to which will do the trick as far as salvation is concerned. But the reality, as we have seen, is that the religious call is not *primarily* a call to sign up to certain metaphysical doctrines, but characteristically and centrally involves a call for moral growth, a demand for righteousness, a challenge to change one's life. The idea of a God who was supremely interested in whether someone had signed on the dotted line and accepted, for example, a particular explication of the exact nature of the Trinity, or a specific account of the precise metaphysics of the Transubstantiation, is clearly contradictory: it attributes to the deity of supposed supreme love and mercy the pettiness of the Stalinist bureaucrat. This is not to disparage the doctrines in question, or to deny that the devout Christian will be wholly committed to them, or some of them, at the centre of their regular praxis of worship and liturgy. But if they have taken the slightest notice of the sayings of the founder of the religion, they will also be acutely aware that 'Not everyone who says to me "Lord!, Lord!" will enter the kingdom of heaven.' This saying, and its context, is enough to repudiate the grotesque idea that participating in the liturgy of some particular denomination will *automatically* get one a better place in the queue for heaven. Those who fail to help the needy, the hungry, the sick, the imprisoned, are, for all their piety and devoutness, chillingly dismissed: 'Depart from me; I never knew you!'[11]

Of course, religious devotion needs, absolutely requires, a vehicle; and believers will legitimately have faith in their forms of worship, and engage in them with love and exaltation and joy, and try to bring others to join them. For Catholics and others, for example, participation in some of those acts of worship, notably the Mass, will be seen as among their strongest obligations, since (among other things) it is believed to be a fulfilment of Christ's commands.[12] Nothing whatever so far said should be taken to detract from the preciousness of such rites, or their genuine efficacy in the believer's growth towards knowledge and love of God. As the philosopher Elizabeth Anscombe aptly puts it in discussing the doctrine of the Transubstantiation in the Eucharist, the food that Christ identified himself with is 'the food of the divine life which is promised and started in us; the viaticum of our perpetual flight from Egypt which is the bondage of sin; the sacrificial offering

[11] Matthew 7:21.
[12] Luke 22:19; cf. 1 Corinthians 11:22.

by which we were reconciled; the sign of our unity with one another in him; the mystery of the faith which is the same for the simple and the learned'.[13]

But equally, no true believer could possibly maintain that attendance at such events is, in itself, either a necessary or a sufficient condition for salvation. It cannot be sufficient, for the reasons just given – nothing overrides or displaces the necessity of the requirement to help the afflicted. ('Not every one who says to me "Lord, Lord" . . .') As to whether it is necessary, we need to be careful. For the believer for whom participation in the Eucharist is the sustaining focus of their moral and spiritual life, being cut off from that source of grace may indeed remove the life-support system that nourishes their faith. Yet that is not at all the same as saying that those who, for whatever cultural or historical reasons, are outside the relevant liturgical circle cannot be saved. Despite the lamentable history of clerical condemnations of 'infidels', and overbearing human attempts to force those of different faiths, or even different denominations, to conform to the rites of the one true way, or to insist that there is 'no salvation outside the Church',[14] the core teaching of Christ is, once again, unequivocal: 'Judge not, that ye be not judged.' It is a monstrous arrogance to take it upon oneself to decide which of one's fellow human beings, in virtue of their ecclesial allegiance or its absence, is or is not fit for salvation. This does not entail a flabby liberalism in which

---

[13] 'On Transubstantiation' [1974].

[14] '*Salus extra ecclesiam non est*.' Augustine of Hippo, *On Baptism* [400], IV, xvii, 24. Compare Acts 4:12.

anything goes; for to be sure, the Christian outlook does imply a stable moral framework, and also the truth of the 'Last Judgement' – that everyone is ultimately held to account for their actions. But judgement means that each person will be required to give an account of the integrity of their *own* life and actions, not to pass a verdict on the life and actions of others.

3. Ultimate responsibility

The question of accountability forms a convenient transition to the second of our prevailing images of the religious outlook:

(B) 'Although science shows our actions to be determined by our genetic inheritance and our environment, religious believers cling to an outmoded notion of "ultimate" responsibility, and the cruel idea of a final judgement leading to eternal bliss or eternal damnation.'

In line with the general strategy of this book, I will address the accuracy of this conception by speaking about the Christian religion, rather than pontificating about other faiths of which I have less knowledge. Christianity certainly maintains as one of its core credal doctrines the idea of the Last Judgement, and, in the form which that doctrine takes, it does clearly presuppose the falsity of a certain type of causal determinism with respect to human behaviour. For (as theists and atheists will all agree) it would be monstrously unfair to pass ultimate judgement on someone if their actions were the inevitable result of genes plus environment. Yet for all that, the idea of 'ultimate' responsibility certainly cannot be dismissed as 'outmoded', for reasons that have already been hinted at at the close of the previous paragraph. I may not be in a position to pass ultimate judgement on *you*, because I simply do not know with certainty the precise structure of your innate predispositions and how they have meshed with your early upbringing and later development to bring you to your present situation, or how strongly that present situation influences your choices. But a wholly deterministic framework, however persuasive it may possibly sometimes seem to be when applied to the actions of others, cannot in good faith be applied to all of my *own* behaviour.

Of course it is true for me also that there may sometimes be hidden causes of my actions. But there remain central and straightforward cases of the exercise of choice where my freedom is absolutely transparent and undeniable. I may not like it, I may try to wriggle out of it with a host of explanations and evasions, but I know perfectly well when I pass the charity worker holding out his tin in the street that nothing is forcing me either to stop or to walk on by. Unless I am drugged or hypnotized or paralysed or otherwise incapacitated, I know with complete certainty, with as much certainty as anything can be known, that I do indeed have this simple 'two-way' power: I am able to reach in my pocket and drop money into the tin, or else to keep the money for some other use. And which I do is up to me. Unless I have an urgent and morally legitimate reason for continuing on my way, my failure to give what I can afford is something for which, like every single choice in my responsible adult life, I must be held to account. My human dignity requires it; the objectivity and inescapability of morality demand it; my deepest reflective impulses of compassion for a fellow-creature convict me of a failure of humanity if I evade it.

To know that one has often failed here is, of course, dreadful; to know that one has no recourse but to ask for mercy is truly devastating to our pride. But the underlying truth of the core idea of ultimate responsibility is not undermined by our being reluctant to accept it. The moral demand, with all its consequences, remains; and theism here is truer and more honest in accepting the ultimacy of this demand than many of the cosier evasions of contemporary naturalism. As Portia uncompromisingly puts it in *The Merchant of Venice*:

> We do pray for mercy
> And that same prayer should teach us all to render
> The deeds of mercy.[15]

But doesn't which choice I make depend on my character, which I can't help? Again, that evasion will not work. Or rather, I may aptly apply it to others (for example, if I can see dreadful circumstances in their early lives that did not allow their moral character to develop properly), but I cannot in good faith apply it to myself. One does not have to be a Christian, or even a theist, to agree with the longstanding consensus starting with Aristotle in the fourth century before Christ, and running right down to Jean-Paul Sartre in the 1940s, that we continuously shape our characters by the choices we make.[16] That does not

---

15 William Shakespeare, *The Merchant of Venice* [*c.* 1597], Act IV, scene 1.

16 Aristotle, *Nicomachean Ethics* [325 BC], Bk III, Ch. 5; Jean-Paul Sartre, *Being and Nothingness* [1943], Part IV, Ch. 2.

mean I am necessarily to be condemned for every charitable appeal I refuse; but it does mean that I can in principle be called to account for this and every single act I perform or fail to perform in the course of my responsible adult life. To abdicate or attempt to abdicate that responsibility is in the end something I cannot in good faith do. And being held to account, ultimately held to account, is simply the corollary of that.

The religious notion of the possibility of *final* and irrevocable divine condemnation at the Last Judgement is admittedly a harder one. But (as many theologians have pointed out) freedom, if it is to be worth anything, cannot be conditional. If we have the power to pursue the good, or its opposite, we must have the power ultimately to reject the good, with all the consequences that entails. But the final judgement is not ours to make: it is not for me to take sides on whether others might be condemned for their behaviour, but simply to accept the inescapability of my own responsibility. One is reminded of a favourite dictum of the late broadcaster and parish priest Dr Cormac Rigby: 'There is only one person about whom I ought to worry whether they are in danger of going to Hell, and that is the person who is speaking these words.'[17] And here it is perhaps worth adding, if the alleged *harshness* of the idea of final condemnation is supposed to be the problem, that one may at least take some comfort from the fact that the judgement itself is, under the Christian worldview, the specific prerogative of Christ. As the letter to the Hebrews puts it, 'For we do not have

[17] See Cormac Rigby, *The Lord Be With You*, p. 81.

a high priest who is unable to sympathize with our weaknesses. Instead, we have one who in every respect has been tempted as we are . . .'[18] Or in the words of a modern theologian, 'It is not simply, as one might expect, God – the infinite, the Unknown, the Eternal – who judges us . . . The judge will not advance to meet us as the entirely Other, but as one of us, who knows human existence from the inside and has suffered.'[19]

4. Souls and the afterlife

I come now to the third and last in our list of widely held summary negative verdicts on the Christian framework of belief:

> (C) *'Christianity is an otherworldly religion, which ignores the problems of this world in the improbable hope of an afterlife. And the afterlife idea requires belief in immaterial souls, whereas modern science has shown that consciousness is physically based.'*

The image of Christianity presented here involves several different elements, all of which involve questionable assessments of its belief structure. In the first place, the charge of 'ignoring the problems of this world' is a grotesque caricature. Those who travel in underprivileged parts of the world are often

---

[18] Hebrews 4:15.
[19] Joseph Ratzinger, *Introduction to Christianity* [1968, rev. 2000] trans. J. Forster, p. 327.

struck by the disproportionate role of Christian organizations in helping the sick and the afflicted, and this concern for the vulnerable has always been a key feature of the Christian ethic. Second, the idea that the Christian worldview advocates a passive attitude of waiting for everything to be put right in some future state is again utterly at variance with what can (in one sense) be called its 'humanocentric' outlook – its affirmation that because of intermingling of the divine and human worlds in the Incarnation, our own human nature can be raised up to its true fulfilment, in a life that strives to be lived in imitation of Christ. And the energetic pursuit of such a life, with the help of all the tools of human ingenuity, technology and science, is precisely what the Christian ideology envisages:

> Christians are convinced that the triumphs of the human race are a sign of God's grace and the flowering of His own mysterious design. For the greater man's power becomes, the farther his individual and community responsibility extends. Hence it is clear that men are not deterred by the Christian message from building up the world, or impelled to neglect the welfare of their fellows, but that they are rather more stringently bound to do these very things.[20]

As for the worry about the idea of the immaterial 'soul' and its supposed incompatibility with modern science, there is again a cluster of misapprehensions that needs to be dispelled.

---

[20] *Gaudium et spes*, Second Vatican Council Document [1965], §34.

In the first place, the Christian Creeds do not, as this criticism implies, talk about the survival into the next world of a Cartesian-style, immaterial soul, but rather speak of the Resurrection of the *body* (in Greek *soma*). This has traditionally been understood as our present human body (as the Fourth Lateran Council put it in 1215, 'All men will rise again with their own bodies which they now bear about them'); but St Paul talks in one place of a transformed 'glorious body',[21] and in another place he speaks in a way that suggests it need not necessarily be understood as this familiar carbon-and-water-based body, but rather as a *soma pneumatikon* or 'spiritual body' – still a body (*soma*), but something distinct from our ordinary human *soma psychikon*, or 'biological body'.[22] So if, along with many modern scientists, you think that a physical substrate of some kind must be required for consciousness to occur, then this would not, *in itself*, be any argument against the possibility of God's preserving an individual human life by providing it with a new *soma*, a new kind of bodily substrate (albeit very different from the body that 'worms will destroy').[23]

Some may object that if this biological body of mine is destroyed, then any subsequent conscious entity inhabiting a new

---

[21] He will 'change the body of our lowliness to make it conformable (*symmorphon*) with the body of his glory', Philippians 3:21.

[22] 1 Corinthians 15:42–44: 'So also is the resurrection of the dead. It is sown in corruption, yet raised in incorruption . . . It is sown a biological body [*soma psychikon*] and raised a spiritual body [*soma pneumatikon*].' See further, J. Cottingham, 'Cartesian dualism: theology, metaphysics, and science' [1992].

[23] 'Though worms destroy this body, yet in the flesh shall I see God' (Job 19:26); note that the language applied to the afterlife is still corporeal ('flesh').

or different kind of body could not really be *me*. This broaches
an extremely vexed philosophical issue; but there is a substantial number of contemporary philosophers who hold that
physical continuity is not necessary for the preservation of
consciousness; what matters, rather, is psychological continuity
or connectedness – what one might call continuity of *informa-
tional content*, rather than concrete molecular continuity.[24]
After all, we are now quite familiar with the idea that informa-
tional content and function can be preserved despite a change
of hardware. Artificial implants containing computer chips can
replace crucial bits of the ear, while preserving the hearing
function; and we may reasonably envisage that damaged parts
of your brain could be replaced by computerized circuits, or
perhaps more sophisticated newly grown synthetic materials,
without loss of the continuing conscious being that is *you*.
These ideas are relatively new and controversial, but their
'functionalist' (as opposed to crudely materialist) framework
actually goes back to Aristotle, who regarded the 'soul' [*psyche*]
as simply the 'form' of the body – not a mysterious Cartesian
substance, but rather the way the bodily organs were *organized*,
so as to be able to perform various mental functions of a
person (such as sensing and feeling).[25] The jury is still out on
what is the correct philosophical theory of the mind, but few
now accept the crude equation of mental states with brain
states that attracted support for a time in the middle decades of
the twentieth century. So whatever your view on these matters,

---

[24] Derek Parfit, *Reasons and Persons* [1984], §§95 and 96.
[25] Aristotle, *De anima* [*c.* 325 BC], Book I, Chs 1 and 4; Book II, Chs 1–3.

it should at least be plain that it simply will not do to issue a blanket dismissal of the Christian framework on the grounds that it invokes a supposedly unscientific idea of how consciousness might be preserved after the death of this biological body.

The idea that psychological connectedness, rather than physical continuity, is what matters in survival, is associated with the views of the British philosopher Derek Parfit. Parfit, however, argues that since such connectedness is a matter of *degree* rather than an all-or-nothing matter (the chains of memory which link different conscious episodes may be more or less strong), it follows that the traditional question of personal identity – of whether what survives will truly be *me* – does not after all matter very much. The conclusion this leads him to is something like the view found among many Buddhists – that the idea of a unique *me*, a core self whose identity is preserved as long as I endure as a person, is an illusion or a fiction.

Here at last there is a strong contrast with the central tenets of Christianity (compared with what we have seen in the case of many of the misapprehensions discussed above). Christian belief is irreducibly individualistic, not in an egoistical sense, but in the sense that it regards each human being as unique and special, and holds that there is a core self which, despite all the physical and psychological changes we undergo during life, remains. Accountability and the possibility of judgement would (as John Locke observed in the seventeenth century)[26]

---

[26] John Locke, *An Essay Concerning Human Understanding* [1690], Book II, Ch. 27, §§22–6.

make no sense without this strong conception of personal identity. But its most important dimension, as with so many aspects of religion that we have been discussing in this book, concerns the moral and spiritual *meaning* of a human life. In the Christian worldview, the whole of creation is brought into being out of love; and the infinite concern of the creator is extended to every one of us. The world we inhabit is not an impersonal world, not a world of meaningless flux where conditions arise and pass away, and where selfhood is an illusion, but a world in which it is truly said even of the sparrow, sold in the market place for two farthings, that 'not one is forgotten before God'. It is a world in which we are told 'not to be afraid, for the very hairs of your head are numbered'.[27] This is the source of the exaltation and hope which, however hard it may sometimes be, the believer is urged to hold on to; it is this which makes learning to believe not merely an intellectual exercise but something which, if the promise of faith is true, will open the door to the 'joy which no man taketh from you'.[28] As to how, given all the problems of human existence, that is supposed to work in the life of the believer, this will be the subject of our final chapter.

---

[27] Luke 12:7.
[28] John 16:22.

Chapter 7

Believing and Living

> *The world in which we live is an artefact brought into being by God. It represents a success on the part of God – God who is love – not a failure. In contemplation of what he had made, God found delight . . . So God pronounced his 'Yes' upon it all, a 'Yes' of delight and of love. You and I must do no less.*
>
> Nicholas Wolterstorff[1]

1. Providence and suffering

The vision of a loving, providential universe which emerged at the end of the last chapter may seem to be fiercely at odds with reality. For even if one grants the claims that were made in Chapter 2 about the beauty and goodness that abound in the natural world, is there not also a great deal that is horrible, painful and ugly? Is it not absurd, even insulting to the victims of the vast amount of pain and distress that we see around us

---

[1] N. Wolterstorff, *Art in Action* [1980], p. 69; cited in Mark Wynn, *Faith and Place* [2009], Ch. 8.

every day, to insist that all this is under the control of an all-powerful and supremely loving God?

Here we come to the problem of suffering, one of the most persistent obstacles to belief in God, and a topic on which more ink has probably been spilt by philosophers and theologians than on any other aspect of religious belief. It is generally known as the 'problem of evil', though the label is not very appropriate, since it is taken to include not only the suffering caused by evil human acts, but also the host of natural ills (disease, floods, earthquakes) which beset us. It would be inept and distasteful to offer, in the closing chapter of a short book, an attempt to solve or 'wrap up' an enigma that has caused so much anguish over the centuries. Indeed, I shall suggest in a moment that it is not in the end feasible to expect a philosophical 'solution', whatever that might be. But first it may be worth recapitulating a few significant points, some very familiar from the literature of 'theodicy' (the attempt to vindicate the goodness and justice of God in the face of the terrible facts of human suffering), and some which seem relatively overlooked.

We must start from the nature of the universe as we find it. And that whole magnificent array is produced by a constant process of decay and destruction. Hydrogen atoms, fused under unimaginable pressures, decay into helium – without this there would be no stars, no light, no warmth. Suns sometimes become unstable and explode in cataclysmic bursts of destruction – without this there would be no heavier elements, out of which the planets and our own bodies are made. And the process of life itself, from the cellular level to the level of organisms and even whole eco-systems, is a constant battle of energies, as animals and plants destroy each other, and in turn decay or are consumed in the ceaseless struggle for existence (something Darwin of course used as a major plank of his theory of evolution, but which many earlier thinkers, such as Schopenhauer, had underlined).[2] 'All things which are bounded with time', as the seventeenth-century philosopher Anne Conway aptly observed, 'are subject to death and corruption, or are changed in to another species of things, as we see water changed into stones, stones into earth, earth into trees, and trees into animals or living creatures.'[3] We humans, the *dust of the earth* as Genesis calls us, *are part of this process.* So it is inherent to our very existence as material, biological beings that we are caught up in the flux of growth, and its inevitable corollary, decay and suffering.[4]

Some creatures of course (plants for example, which lack a central nervous system) are part of the process yet without the suffering. Yet the price for that is lack of any consciousness whatsoever. Conscious beings, made of unstable elements as we are, and vulnerable to countless resulting accidents and dangers, must have pain mechanisms to alert us to those dangers – otherwise we would not survive a minute. Human life, or anything remotely like it, cannot be pain free.

---

[2] Charles Darwin, *On the Origin of Species* [1859], *passim*; Arthur Schopenhauer, *The World and Will and Representation* [1818], Book II, Ch. 28; trans. E. F. J. Payne, Part ii, p. 354.

[3] Anne Conway, *The Principles of the Most Ancient and Modern Philosophy* [1690], Ch. 5, §6; repr. in Taliaferro and Teply (eds), *Cambridge Platonist Spirituality*, p. 191.

[4] See J. Cottingham, *The Spiritual Dimension*, Ch. 2, §3.

Yet why does not God intervene to stop the worst results of this inexorable process? As we saw in Chapter 4, nothing in science logically precludes the notion of supernatural intervention – so why, if there is a God, does he not do more of it? There are some familiar answers in the theodicy literature: a great deal of suffering (perhaps the most terrible kind) is caused by the free actions of humans, and since freedom is a great good, something we would never give up, we can see how a loving God would choose to bestow it, terrible as the cost often is. But that answer is not enough: for there is some suffering so extreme, so excessive, that we are quite sure that even an imperfectly and inadequately loving human being, let alone a God, would restrict the free action that caused it, if they could; so the charge against the deity, who is supposed to know how bad things are, and to have the power to stop them, is not so easily rebutted.

Suffering, to be sure, is vital to moral growth – a point that the poet Keats made when he said that this 'vale of tears' should better be called a 'vale of soul-making'.[5] The slow and hard experience of life makes it plain that the greatest good in human life, love, is inextricably bound up with the kind of caring that is prepared to risk the pain of loss. A love that is totally comfortable and secure, free from any risk of loss or rejection, free from any danger of accident or division, would not have a

---

[5] See John Keats, letter to George and Georgina Keats of spring 1819: 'The common cognomen of this world among the misguided and superstitious is "a vale of tears", from which we are to be redeemed by a certain arbitrary interposition of God and taken to Heaven – what a little circumscribe[d] straightened notion! Call the world if you Please "The vale of Soul-making".'

hundredth part of the depth and the tenderness that is plumbed by the human heart at its most vulnerable. The ancient message that the psychologist Carl Jung distilled from the Gospels, 'Give up what thou hast and then thou wilt receive',[6] perhaps encapsulates as well as anything this hard fact, that the law of love is the law of sacrifice. Or as T. S. Eliot put it in the 'Four Quartets':

> Who then devised the torment? Love.
> Love is the unfamiliar Name
> Behind the hands that wove
> The intolerable shirt of flame
> Which human power cannot remove.[7]

Yet for all that, and despite the strength and complexity of the link between love and sacrifice, there is no complete 'solution' here to the problem of evil – no solution, that is, which will embrace the *excess*, the superfluity of suffering we clearly find in the world, beyond any that could conceivably be required for moral development or the flowering of the deepest kind of love.

---

[6] 'Until a person . . . at some time, at whatever cost to his pride, ceases to defend and assert himself, and . . . can confess himself fallible and human, an impenetrable wall shuts him out from the living experience of feeling himself a man among men. Here we find the key to the great significance of . . . the saying "Give up what thou hast, and then thou wilt receive".' C. Jung, 'Problems of Modern Psychotherapy' [1931], in *Modern Man in Search of a Soul*, Ch. 2, p. 40.

[7] T. S. Eliot, 'Little Gidding' [1942], lines 207–11; in *Four Quartets* (London: Faber, 1959).

At this point, I think, philosophical argument must come to an end. The opponents of theism may devise ever more dramatic presentations of the problem of evil, and its defenders construct ever more ingenious rebuttals, but one has the sense that neither side in the argument has any real expectation of changing their opponent's mind, and that in the end they are succeeding in doing little more than upsetting each other. Part of the reason for this has been articulated by the philosopher Alvin Plantinga, an exponent of the most meticulous analytic philosophy, who has made seminal contributions to the intellectual debate over the problem of evil, yet whose most recent observations seem to acknowledge that there is a point at which rational discussion must run out of steam. The believer, argues Plantinga, is one whose faith is firmly grounded in a *sensus divinitatis*, a vivid sense of the presence of God in the world. Such a person may be appalled at the horrifying evils the world contains, deeply perplexed at God's role in permitting them, perhaps even angry and resentful; but 'needn't entertain for a moment the belief that there is no such person as God'. When God appears to Job out of the whirlwind, 'the point is not really to convince him that God has his reasons, but to quiet him, to still the storm in his soul . . . [so that] the doubts and turmoil abate and once more Job loves and trusts the Lord'.[8]

Such are the struggles of religious belief. They may be won or lost, but the terrain on which the battle will be fought will

---

[8] In Alvin Plantinga and Michael Tooley, *Knowledge of God*, p. 183. Cf. Job, Chs 40–42.

always in the end be a moral and spiritual and existential one, and it can never be circumvented by taking the path of logic and evidence alone, however carefully that path is followed. What faith offers is not a demonstrative or even a probabilistic solution to the problem of the amount and degree of suffering found in the world, but a resolve never to abandon the struggle to follow the path of love. The resounding words of encouragement St Paul offered to his fellow believers are powerfully relevant here, precisely because they do *not* claim to provide a solution, but because they point instead to the transforming power of that love, so strong that 'neither hardship, nor distress, nor persecution, nor famine nor nakedness nor danger nor the sword' can separate us from it. It is not a matter of a balance sheet, not a matter of listing these sufferings as evidence against God's love, and proceeding to offer some countervailing data, but rather of holding fast to an extraordinary conviction – that not *despite* all these things, but *in the midst of* all these things 'we are more than conquerors, through him who loved us'.[9]

2. Humility and hope

Mention of the actual emotional orientation of the believer, one that is characterized by holding on to love and trust in the face of what are often daunting setbacks, brings us to what one might call the *ethical psychology of religious belief* – an area that is often curiously neglected in analytic philosophy of religion,

---

[9] Romans 8:35–37.

with its stress (perfectly legitimate and valuable as far as it goes) on adversarial debate.

If we are looking for attitudes that are distinctive of a religious outlook, it makes sense to start with the classic Christian virtue of humility. From a purely naturalist perspective, it might well be supposed that this is not a virtue at all. It is significant, for example, that it holds no place in Aristotle's schema of the virtues. There is, for Aristotle, the virtue of having a due sense of how much lavishness and external grandeur one's station in life demands, namely *megaloprepeia*, or magnificence; and this virtue is flanked by a corresponding vice of excess – vulgarity or crude self-display – and a vice of deficiency, namely mean-mindedness or pettiness (*microprepeia*). But humility as such, putting oneself last, as enjoined in various Gospel parables, is simply absent from this particular Greek pattern of commendable or deplorable dispositions and attitudes. Moving to a slightly different dimension of the worthwhile life, Aristotle goes on to speak of a distinctive virtue of *proper ambition*, a justified desire to secure the honour that is one's due. This is contrasted with its vice of excess, the tendency (as we might say) to be over-pushy, and on the other hand with its vice of deficiency, an insufficient zeal for honour and fame; but here again there is no way of fitting genuine humility into the schema. Finally, in the sphere of what one says and thinks, as opposed to what one does, Aristotle acknowledges the virtue of *proper self-estimation*, of telling the truth about oneself; this has a vice of excess, boastfulness, but at the other end of the scale we do not have humility, but instead a vice of deficiency called *eironeia*, which is a tiresome disposition to conceal or understate one's due merits; again, humility simply doesn't fit anywhere in this particular scale.[10]

Secular naturalists have a dilemma here, I think. Either they can go along with Aristotle and simply accept a schema of proper human character and conduct that allows no place for humility; or they can acknowledge the moral pull of something like the Christian conception of humility and try to find a secular analogue for it. What exactly is humility then, in the Christian framework of interpretation? First, it is a certain forbearance, a readiness as in the parable, not to stride up to the place of honour, but to take a lower seat, and wait until one may be asked to 'go up higher'.[11] This implies, perhaps, a consciousness of one's own defects, but it also implies a certain purity of character – an inner integrity, a lack of anxious concern to insist on matters of status, a recognition that one is but one among many others, and that one's gifts, if such they be, are not ultimately of one's own making. Religious language offers a ready expression for this complex framework of affective and cognitive responses. Man is not self-creating: 'It is he who hath made us and not we ourselves.' The mighty may 'boast and trust in the abundance of their riches', but the righteous man, though 'poor and needy' is 'like a green olive tree in

---

10 For these various virtues and vices, see Aristotle, *Nicomachean Ethics* [c. 325 BC], Bk IV, esp. Chs 2, 4 and 7. For the general triadic scheme of the virtues, each with a flanking vice of excess and of deficiency, see Bk II, Ch. 8.

11 The parable of the wedding guest: Luke 14:10.

the house of God, trusting in the mercy of God for ever'.[12] The quotations could be multiplied endlessly; and the framework they imply is one in which humility has a recognized and stable place. Remove the framework, and the injunction to be humble can start to look arbitrary and unsupported. For an exhortation to virtue is not just a raw set of prescriptions on how to act, or on what dispositions to cultivate; it necessarily involves a *background of significance,* a wider picture of the goals of human life, or the best way of living. Without such a background picture, any given candidate for a virtue or vice will be isolated from its source of meaning; to change the metaphor, it will be like a plant that grew in a certain soil, which could theoretically be uprooted and transported to a different climate and conditions, but which in reality cannot properly take root and thrive there.

The above quotations referring to humility also serve to introduce another distinctively religious cluster of virtues, those of faith, hope and trust. 'O Israel, *trust* in the Lord,' says the Psalmist, 'for in him there is mercy, and in him is plenteous redemption.' Or again, 'I *hope* for the Lord; my soul doth *wait* for him; in his word is my *trust.*'[13] Again, there is no proper placeholder for these traits in classical virtue theory. On the contrary, one of the characteristic features of ancient Greek

---

[12] For these various quotations, see Psalms 100[99]:3; 49[48]:6; 40[39]:17; 70[69]:5; 52[51]:8. The translation and numbering of chapters is from the King James version and/or the Book of Common Prayer, both of which follow the numbering in the Hebrew Bible; the alternative numbering in square brackets is that of the Vulgate (Latin) and Septuagint (Greek) versions.

[13] Psalm 130[129]:5–7.

thought, both in Aristotle and in the tradition he inherited, was a distinctly sober, not to say gloomy, awareness of how often hopes can be disappointed, of how easily human life can be overturned, even for the most virtuous and prosperous, by the swings of fortune.[14] 'Call no man happy until he is dead', ran the proverb, etched deep into the mindset of most of the philosophers and poets of classical antiquity.[15] But the cry of Job, 'Though he slay me, yet will I trust in him',[16] or St Paul's 'neither height nor depth nor . . . things present nor things to come . . . shall be able to separate us from the love of God',[17] express something quite outside the range of this classical fatalism: an indomitable determination to trust and to keep hope alive, to 'hope against hope', as Paul put it in his letter to the Romans.[18]

Again, I suggest, the naturalist faces a dilemma here. On the one hand, it is hard to deny that there is something admirable about this ethic of hope and trust. And the value is something we seem to recognize not just on a prudential level (though there may be some evidence that people stranded in a lifeboat who can keep their hopes up are more likely to survive for longer than those who despair). Over and above such utilitarian

---

[14] See Aristotle on the terrible misfortunes suffered by King Priam at the end of what had hitherto been a prosperous and happy life: *Nicomachean Ethics*, Bk I, Ch. 10.

[15] The saying is attributed to the ancient lawgiver Solon, but is found, for example, at the end of Sophocles' play *Oedipus Tyrannus* (mid-fifth century BC).

[16] Job 1:4.

[17] Romans 8:38.

[18] Romans 4:18.

considerations, most of us have a strong intuitive sense of something splendid, something moving, about the human being
weighed down with misfortunes and difficulties, who nevertheless manages to keep alive the radiance of hope, as is done in the
straining yet resonant self-exhortation at the end of Psalm 43:
'Why are thou cast down, O my soul, and why are thou disqui-
eted within me? Hope in God for I shall yet praise him who is
the health of my countenance, and my God.'[19]

The position so far reached, then, is that these so-called
theological virtues are ones which many or most of us, almost
irrespective of religious persuasion or its absence, can intuitively recognize as admirable and valuable. And hence, short of
biting the bullet and suppressing such intuitions, the naturalist
has to construct some secular analogue for these virtues, which
will allow them to be preserved as ethically desirable traits of
character. But I have suggested that this will not be easy,
without a suitable framework in which to locate them. A recent
valiant attempt to translate them into a purely secular context
has been made by Erik Wielenberg, in his study *Value and
Virtue in a Godless Universe*. In the secularized schema offered
by Wielenberg, humility becomes a recognition of 'the tremen-
dous contribution *dumb luck* has made to all human accomplishments', so that 'taking the balance of credit for one's
accomplishments is foolish'.[20] The central theological virtue of
hope, maintained in the face of radical vulnerability and the
ever-present human tendency to buckle under external misfor-

---

[19] Psalm 42 in the Vulgate numbering.
[20] E. J. Wielenberg, *Value and Virtue in a Godless Universe*, pp. 110, 112.

tune or internal weakness, becomes for Wielenberg a confidence in the power of science to ameliorate our lot (including by pharmacological means), pointing us towards 'the upper limits of justice and happiness' that 'remain to be discovered'.[21]

What is interesting about these Wielenbergian virtues – recognition of our dependence on fortune, and optimism about the progress of science – is what one might call the 'thinness' of their psychological profile. A judicious assessment of how far one's advantages are due to genetic and environmental contingencies; a carefully argued (but presumably revisable) positive estimate of what can be achieved by scientific advance: these seem more like positions for debate than deeply ingrained dispositions of emotion and action. Without going into whether or not they are worthy beliefs to cultivate, they are not integrated, as the religious virtues are, into a complex psychological story about self-discovery, moral growth through suffering, and what the spiritual writers called *metanoia* (changed awareness). What Wielenberg has given us, I would suggest, are essentially 'static' components of the belief-system characteristic of the rational secular outlook; there may be nothing wrong with this, but what is left out, in the process of constructing the secular analogues, is almost every motivational and psychological aspect of the spiritual life that has made the traditional religious virtues intelligible and attractive to those who aspire to them.

---

21 Wielenberg, *Value and Virtue*, p. 139.

3. Awe and thanksgiving

The starry heavens above and the moral law within were for Immanuel Kant the two principal sources of what he called 'awe' (*Achtung*).[22] A sense of wonder at the grandeur of the universe, the splendour and vastness of the night sky, is something that figures in many ancient religious writings, of which perhaps the best known is the psalm *Caeli enarrant gloriam Dei*, 'The heavens declare the glory of the Lord'.[23] Some atheists have protested sharply at the theist trying to appropriate wonder and awe as part of the religious outlook,[24] but it turns out, as we found in the case of humility and of hope, that it is not particularly easy to construct purely secular analogues of these reactive attitudes. Of course it would be foolish to deny that committed atheists can enjoy a rich and complex aesthetic appreciation of the natural world; one does not need to check someone's religious allegiance, or lack of it, to decide whether they can be having a powerful experience when they look at the sunset over the ocean and say 'Wow!'. But awe implies something rather more than this.

To begin with, there is a link with humility. The contemplation of the vastness of the universe is, as Pascal noted, particularly evocative of the puniness of humankind beside the unbounded cosmic backdrop against which we play out our tiny

---

[22] Immanuel Kant, *Critique of Practical Reason* [1788], Conclusion.

[23] Psalm 19[18].

[24] Cf. Richard Norman, 'The Varieties of Non-Religious Experience', in J. Cottingham (ed.), *The Meaning of Theism*.

existence.[25] But this sense of the cosmic insignificance of humankind is only part of the story. Awe implies more than a sense of fear at something vastly greater than oneself; it also suggests a recognition of the grandeur and splendour of that greater thing – what in the Hebrew Bible is called *kavod*, 'glory'. This term, hard to translate, appears in the first verse of the Psalm just referred to ('The heavens declare the *glory* of God'), and it is interesting to note that the response evoked by such perceived 'glory' is not merely an 'aesthetic' one, in the rather thin modern sense which we sometimes use when referring to the frisson someone may get from looking at a sunset or a beautiful flower. It is a recognition of that which is both magnificent and wondrous in itself, and which also calls to something in our *moral* nature. The same Psalm just cited (one which must certainly have inspired Kant's linkage of the starry heavens above and the moral law within) proceeds directly from acknowledging the 'glory of the Lord', as manifested in the heavens, to extolling the 'law (*torah*) of the Lord', which is described in terms that are no less awestruck: the law of the Lord is perfect, rejoicing the heart, enlightening the eyes, more desired than gold, sweeter than honey. These responses would be very inadequately described as 'aesthetic'; they are, rather, a complete submission of the whole

---

25 'I see these frightening expanses of the universe that shut me in, and I find myself stuck in one corner of this vast emptiness, without knowing why I am placed here rather than elsewhere, or why from out of the whole eternity that has gone before me and the whole eternity that will follow, this one tiny period has been given me in which to live out my life. I see only infinities on every side which shut me in like an atom, like a shadow that lasts only an instant . . .' Blaise Pascal, *Pensées* [c. 1660], ed. Lafuma, no. 427.

mind, intellectual, sensory and moral, to something vastly greater and more perfect than itself, something to which we react with humility and yet with joy, something whose 'glory' is awesome precisely because it is fearfully and wholly good.

Down the centuries, such responses have taken many different forms, shaped by different cultural and historical circumstances, but all speaking to something deep in our humanity. In the poem of William Wordsworth, which we began by referring to in the opening section of Chapter 1, there is something of the same awe:

> I have felt
> A presence that disturbs me with the sense
> Of elevated thoughts; a sense sublime
> Of something far more deeply interfused
> Whose dwelling is the light of setting suns,
> And the round ocean, and the living air
> And the blue sky, and in the mind of man . . .[26]

The language is not, to be sure, overtly theistic, but speculating about the precise metaphysical implications of the sentiments expressed here is in a certain sense beside the point. For the unmistakably religious orientation of the passage depends less on doctrinal commitments than on the characteristic way in which the poet's response fuses together elements of the

---

[26] 'Lines Written a Few Miles Above Tintern Abbey' [1798], lines 89–100. For further discussion of the philosophical significance of this passage, see J. Cottingham, '"Our natural guide . . .": Conscience, "nature" and moral experience'.

aesthetic and the moral, recognizing the goodness and beauty of the cosmos in a way that intimately relates it to human concerns. The vision, once glimpsed, says Wordsworth a few lines later (bringing us back to the lines we quoted in Chapter 1) gives us something that no subsequent pain or distress can entirely erase, a

> cheerful faith that all which we behold
> is full of *blessings*.[27]

The notion of 'blessing' leads me to mention one final disposition or attitude characteristic of the theistic outlook, namely a readiness to see the circumstances of human life, and indeed human life itself, as *gifts* – that is, as fit to evoke responses of thankfulness and praise. This is manifested in many aspects of religious praxis – for example in stylized routines of prayer and praise performed regularly throughout each day. Elaborated examples of this are the obligations of the Divine Office associated in the Christian tradition with specialized religious orders; but a more basic routine, for example of morning and evening prayer, is widely practised by laypeople throughout Christianity and Judaism; and in the form of *Salah*, praying to Allah five times a day, is taken in Islam to be one of the basic duties of every believer.[28] The idea is a simple

---

27 'Tintern Abbey', lines 135–6 (emphasis supplied).

28 *Salah* is the second of the 'five pillars' (*arkan ad-din*) or basic duties of Islam, the others being the *shahadah* (avowal that there is no God but Allah and Muhammad is his prophet); *zakat* (almsgiving); *sawm* (fasting in Ramadan) and *hajj* (pilgrimage to Mecca once in a lifetime). The 'avowal' requirement of course takes us beyond mere praxis.

one: to put it at its most high-minded, the required mindset is that each new day be seen as a blessing, as a gift to be used for the development of one's own talents and for the good of one's fellow human beings. A similar conception underlies the practice of saying Grace at meals, as is brought out by Leonard Kass:

> A blessing offered over the meal still fosters a fitting attitude toward the world, whose gracious bounty is available to us, and not because we merit it . . . The materialistic view of life, though it may help put bread on the table, cannot help us understand what it *means* to eat . . . Recovering the deeper meaning of eating could help [us] . . . see again that living in a needy body is no disgrace and that our particular upright embodiment orients us toward the beautiful, the good, the true and the holy.[29]

It is again difficult not to see something admirable about the practices and attitudes so described; and again the question of whether one should acknowledge their value puts the atheist in a similar kind of dilemma to that which I have posed earlier. To bite the bullet and deny all value to such practices seems harshly out of tune with our intuitions; but to attempt to preserve what is valuable in them while discarding the theistic vehicle in terms of which they are expressed seems doomed to failure, or at least very hard to achieve. One could imagine a zealous humanist trying to construct some secular analogue

---

[29] L. R. Kass, *The Hungry Soul*, pp. 228–31. See further J. Cottingham, *On the Meaning of Life*, pp. 97ff.

for morning prayer, or for Grace before meals. But the most likely result of such endeavours, I predict, will be something flat and indigestible – a formula that merely asserts, 'Well, it's nice that I am still alive for another day of potential activities that may be worthwhile for myself and others'; or 'It's good that we are about to sit down to a nice meal, and it's ethically useful to remember that much work was necessary to enable this nutrition to be made available to us.' It is not that such views are devoid of value, or that it would be pointless to utter them, but that their thinness, their lack of the power and resonance given by a rich interpretative context, means they cannot capture a great deal of what is valuable in their theistic analogues. Just as a sober and unbiased assessment of one's merits leaves out much of what is valuable about the virtue of humility, and just as a purely aesthetic admiration of a fine sunset fails to capture what is meant by a sense of awe, in the same way such 'humanistic' analogues for prayer and praise seem to be woefully lightweight vehicles for carrying the weight of intellectual and affective response conveyed by the formulae of traditional spiritual praxis.

We have by now reached a heterogeneous range of reactive responses – humility, hope, awe, thankfulness – which have been identified as attitudes without which human life would be the poorer. A religious framework of interpretation provides a secure home for these attitudes, by offering vehicles for their systematic and regular expression, and allows them significance by incorporating them into a recognized schema of virtuous praxis. To the objection that the atheist could construct valid secular analogues of these responses, I have replied that such a task, though theoretically possible, carries a serious risk of filtering out precisely what gives them depth and significance. And in practice, it may be added (albeit at the risk of generalizing into risky empirical territory), most atheists are unlikely in the first place to be tempted to investigate the possibility of alternative secularized forms of spiritual praxis. Atheism is most characteristically linked to a 'no-nonsense' rationalistic and sceptical kind of outlook, and a great many of its adherents are likely to condemn or discard the whole notion of spirituality as part of an untenable supernaturalist world picture.[30] So the upshot is that in the absence of morning prayer, one will simply get up in the morning and start the day; in the absence of a habit of saying Grace, one will simply pick up the knife and fork and start eating. These, and many other differences in habitual patterns of behaviour and affective response, often give us a more significant indicator of the difference between atheism and theism than if we focus on the abstract metaphysical claims. So the ultimate answer to our central question, 'Why believe?', or at least a significant part of that answer, is that the mindset of a theist enables him or her

---

[30] A worldview which fits neither in this 'no-nonsense' camp nor in the theistic category is the Buddhist religion, which (in its prevailing form) is nontheistic, yet finds an important place for spiritual praxis. In a recent study sympathetic to the Buddhist outlook, David Cooper speaks of forms of Zen praxis as 'allowing things to be experienced as the "gifts" they are' (*A Philosophy of Gardens*, p. 158). It is unclear, however, how a framework of interpretation that views the world as an impersonal flux could find a genuine place for the kinds of affective response associated with, for example, saying Grace: it is significant that Cooper feels obliged, in the passage just cited, to put the word 'gifts' in inverted commas.

to approach the task of living with a characteristic framework of hermeneusis and praxis, a framework that, though not scientifically demonstrable, is at least consistent with anything science can tell us, a framework which finds room for some of our deepest and most valuable human impulses, and which there is therefore strong reason to regard as enriching the life of those who adopt it.

4. 'Walk the believer's road!'

We have argued in the previous two sections that the religious framework provides a conceptual home for the morally admirable qualities of hope and humility, and for our deep impulse to respond to the gifts of life with thankfulness and awe. But to say that religious belief provides a 'conceptual home' for these dispositions is of course not at all the same as saying that religious adherents will always display the relevant qualities in their words and actions. Indeed, if we consider the moral life generally, it is all too apparent that membership of a religious group is neither necessary for, nor does it guarantee, virtuous behaviour. This perhaps just needs saying, given that one of the things that justifiably irritates non-believers is the 'holier than thou' attitude sometimes adopted by religious people – the idea that their inner life and outward conduct are somehow on a higher plane than that of their secular counterparts.

Such smug claims to superiority need to be decisively repudiated. Cliché though it may be to say 'Some of my best friends are *xxxx*' (fill in an appropriate group of 'outsiders'), in our mingled and heterogeneous modern society, friendship that genuinely reaches across religious and other barriers is something exceedingly precious; and a readiness to recognize the merits of those with different core beliefs is vitally important. Few but the most insular of religious believers will fail to acknowledge they know people of different faiths, or of no faith, who often greatly surpass them in kindness and generosity and thoughtfulness, and so on down the catalogue of virtues. Religious and moral impulses are intimately interlinked – that has been one of the central messages of this book. But not, emphatically not, in a way that implies that the former are either a necessary or sufficient condition for the latter.

Believers should not claim to be 'holier than thou'. And neither should they claim to be 'more enlightened than thou', if by that is meant that they have access to a better set of explanatory hypotheses than their secular colleagues. For religious beliefs are *not* in any normal sense explanatory hypotheses at all. As Anthony Kenny has aptly observed:

> The way in which God accounts for the unexplained is not by figuring in some further explanation. When we invoke God we do not explain the world, or any series of phenomena in the world. The mode of intelligibility which is provided by the invocation of God is something of quite different kind . . . The concept of God provides not explanation but *understanding*.[31]

---

[31] Anthony Kenny, *What is Faith?*, p. 112; emphasis supplied.

It is for this reason that the current batch of sparring between Dawkinsites and fundamentalists, about 'creationism' versus Darwinism, or whether 'the God hypothesis' (as Dawkins calls it) provides a better explanation than the theory of evolution, is utterly sterile and pointless.[32] Religious believers may or may not be scientists (and there is no reason whatever why they should not be); but *qua* religious believers they are not in the business doing alternative science, but of 'understanding' – interpreting the moral and spiritual significance of the world. To suppose that this is in conflict with using the best gifts of reason and observation to investigate the structure and workings of the world is a radical confusion. Since theists view the world as brought into being (via whatever mechanisms or processes) by the creative power of God, they will, as we have seen, have a distinctive response to certain features of the world (its beauty, its goodness, its wonder);[33] but none of this precludes, or is in competition with, the valuable process of exploring the nature and origins of the world by the best and most rigorous methods of natural science.

The believer, then, cannot claim to have a special passport to moral purity, or a special passport to scientific truth. In both cases, there are no religious 'short cuts': human beings have to use their natural gifts, the gifts of reason and reflection and careful observation, to try as best they can to discern the truth, whether in the scientific or the ethical realm. All this puts the believer and the non-believer very much in the same category

---

[32] See Richard Dawkins, *The God Delusion*, *passim*.
[33] See Chapter 2, above, and Section 3 of the present chapter.

when it comes to formulating the best account we can of the natural world, and of the proper social and ethical structures for the conduct of life.

So where does this leave religious belief? What difference does it make? What is it, in the end, to walk the believer's road? I hope that a large part of the answer will have emerged already, from our discussions of how taking such a path accommodates and integrates our deepest human sensibilities (Chapter 1); of how it provides a rich and satisfying understanding of the value with which reality is imbued (Chapter 2); of how it enables us to reach beyond an ultimately meaningless 'closed' cosmos towards the transcendent (Chapter 3); of how it is guided by supernaturalist framework that is not after all contradicted by science (Chapter 4); of how it gains sustenance and momentum from an emotional and moral transformation which allows meaning to be disclosed (Chapter 5); of how it is not something decided on as a result of carefully assessed evidence but urged upon us through the hard lessons of life (Chapter 6).

But what religious belief amounts to, in the life of the believer, is nevertheless not something that can easily be defined philosophically, or analysed through the intellect alone. Its tone, its dynamic, is perhaps in the end best conveyed by something that partly transcends words; and so it may be appropriate to close this final chapter by referring to a musical work that both describes and advocates taking the believer's path – J. S. Bach's cantata, *Tritt auf die Glaubensbahn* (BWV 152). First performed in 1714, this short but remarkable composition for voice and instruments lifts us, as so often with Bach's music, into a dimension of spirituality which does not *state*, but rather *shows*, through the weaving of the text into the harmonic and contrapuntal and melodic texture of the music, something of what the religious orientation amounts to.

The words of the opening aria are themselves highly significant. *Tritt auf die Glaubensbahn*: 'Walk the believer's road!', or, perhaps better, 'Tread firm the path of faith!'[34] It is an injunction, not a statement; and what we are enjoined to do is not to examine a doctrine, but to set out on a new path of life. For, aptly enough, Christianity at its earliest origins was known not as 'The Teaching' but as 'The Way'.[35] And here, in the music, there is no smug self-confidence about one's superior doctrines or one's moral credentials, no arrogant claim to have done better than science, no exclusivist triumphalism over one's fellow creatures of different persuasions and different paths. Rather, there is the steady, rhythmical support of the viola da

---

[34] The lyrics run as follows:

Tritt auf die Glaubensbahn,
Gott hat den Stein geleget,
Der Zion hält und träget,
Mensch, stoße dich nicht dran!
Tritt auf die Glaubensbahn!

An approximate rendering, preserving the rhyme scheme and metre, might be:

Tread the believer's way.
God laid the strong foundation,
The rock of Sion's salvation;
Man, stumble not, nor stray!
Tread the believer's way!

[35] See, for example, Acts 24:22.

gamba, marking out the beat of the journey, and the plaintive, vulnerable tones of the oboe, soaring up and down, in haunting cadences, as if to signal the heights and depths of human joy and suffering that await us as the journey unfolds. And above all, the firmness and resolve of the bass singing line – not the ethereal soprano voice, or the exalted tones of the tenor, but a steady, down-to-earth and deeply human encouragement, solid and undaunted, rising and falling, yet returning again and again to the refrain that announces the continuing task: 'Tread firm the path of faith!' 'Walk the believer's road!'

There is no promise that it will be easy. But this much, if we knew anything of human life, we knew already. There is no guarantee of the outcome, for though the road is partly lit by reason, it is built on faith. And humility permits no impugning of those who take a different route. But for some, as long as the music of our human longing calls us, as long as we remain true to the entirety of what our understanding discloses, there will be no other path we can with integrity follow.

Bibliography

Anscombe, Elizabeth, 'On Transubstantiation' [1974], in G. E. M. Anscombe, *Faith in a Hard Ground: Essays in Religion, Politics and Ethics*, ed. M. Geach and L. Gormally (St Andrews: Imprint Academic, 2008).

Anselm of Canterbury, *Proslogion* [1077–8], in *The Major Works*, ed. B. Davies and G. R. Evans (Oxford: Oxford University Press, 1998).

Aquinas, Thomas, *Summa theologiae* [1266–73], trans. Fathers of the English Dominican Province (London: Burns, Oates and Washbourne, 1911).

Aristotle, *De anima* [*c.* 325 BC], ed. and transl. D. W. Hamlyn (Oxford: Clarendon, 1968).

Aristotle, *Metaphysics* [*c.* 325 BC], trans. H. Tredennick (Cambridge, Mass.: Harvard University Press, 1989).

Aristotle, *Nicomachean Ethics* [325 BC], ed. T. Irwin (Indianapolis, Ind.: Hackett, 1985).

Augustine of Hippo, *Confessions* [*Confessiones, c.* 398], trans. W. Watts (Cambridge, Mass.: Harvard University Press, 1912).

Augustine of Hippo, *On Baptism* [*De Baptismo contra Donatistas*, 400], *On the Benefits of Believing* [*De utilitate credendi*, 392], *Commentary on Genesis* [*De Genesi ad litteram*, 401–14], *On Nature and Grace* [*De natura et gratia*, 415], *Sermons* [*Sermones*, 392–430], *On True Religion* [*De vera religione*, 391]; in J. Migne (ed.), *Patrologia Latina* (Paris, 1857–66).

Aurelius, Marcus, *Meditations* [*Ta eis heauton*, c. AD 85] trans. M. Hammond (Harmondsworth: Penguin, 1995).

Benedict XVI, *Deus Caritas Est* [Encyclical letter, 2005]; http://www.vatican.va/holy_father/benedict_xvi/encyclicals/documents/

Bultmann, R. K., 'Neues Testament und Mythologie: Das Problem der Entmythologisierung der neutestamentichen Verkündigen' [1941], trans. in S. M. Ogden (Minneapolis, Minn.: Augsburg Fortress: 1990).

Bunyan, John, *The Pilgrim's Progress* [1678], ed. J. B. Wharey and R. Sharrock (Oxford: Clarendon Press, 2nd edn, 1960).

Camus, Albert, *Le Mythe de Sisyphe* (Paris: Gallimard, 1942), trans. *The Myth of Sisyphus*, J. O'Brien (London: Penguin, 2000).

Coakley, Sarah, *Powers and Submissions: Spirituality, Philosophy and Gender* (Oxford: Blackwell, 2002).

Conway, Anne, *The Principles of the Most Ancient and Modern Philosophy* [1690], extracts repr. in C. Taliaferro and A. J. Teply (eds), *Cambridge Platonist Spirituality*.

Cooper, David, *A Philosophy of Gardens* (Oxford: Oxford University Press, 2005).

Cottingham, John, 'Cartesian Dualism: Theology, Metaphysics, and

Science', in Cottingham (ed.), *The Cambridge Companion to Descartes* (Cambridge: Cambridge University Press, 1992), Ch. 8.

Cottingham, John, *Cartesian Reflections* (Oxford: Oxford University Press, 2008).

Cottingham, John, *On the Meaning of Life* (London: Routledge, 2003).

Cottingham, John, '"Our natural guide . . .": Conscience, "Nature" and Moral Experience', in D. S. Oderberg and T. Chappell (eds), *Human Values: New Essays on Ethics and Natural Law* (London: Palgrave, 2005), pp. 11–31.

Cottingham, John, *Philosophy and the Good Life: Reason and the Passions in Greek, Cartesian and Psychoanalytic Ethics* (Cambridge: Cambridge University Press, 1998).

Cottingham, John, 'The Lessons of Life: Wittgenstein, Religion and Analytic Philosophy', in J. Hyman and H.-J. Glock (eds), *Wittgenstein and Twentieth-Century Analytic Philosophy: Essays in Honour of P. M. S. Hacker* (Oxford: Oxford University Press, 2009), pp. 203–27.

Cottingham, John, *The Rationalists* (Oxford: Oxford University Press, 1988).

Cottingham, John, *The Spiritual Dimension* (Cambridge: Cambridge University Press, 2005).

Cottingham, John, 'What Difference Does It Make? The Nature and Significance of Theistic Belief', *Ratio* XIX (4), December 2006, pp. 401–20; repr. in Cottingham (ed.), *The Meaning of Theism*.

Cottingham, John, 'What is Humane Philosophy and Why is it at Risk?', in A. O'Hear (ed.), *Conceptions of Philosophy*, Royal

Institute of Philosophy series (Cambridge: Cambridge University Press, 2009).

Cottingham, John (ed.), *The Meaning of Theism* (Oxford: Blackwell, 2007).

Cupitt, Don, *The Sea of Faith* (London: BBC Books, 1984).

Cupitt, Don, *Taking Leave of God* [1980] (London: SCM Press, 2001).

Dalferth, Ingolf, 'Self-Sacrifice: From the Act of Violence to the Passion of Love', typescript (2008). Paper delivered at European Society for the Philosophy of Religion Conference, University of Oslo, September 2008.

Darwin, Charles, *On the Origin of Species* [1859], ed. J. W. Burrow (Harmondsworth: Penguin, 1968).

Davies, B., *Aquinas* (London: Continuum, 2002).

Dawkins, Richard, *The God Delusion* (London: Bantam Press, 2006).

Descartes, René, *Discourse on the Method* [*Discours de la méthode*, 1637], trans. in J. Cottingham, R. Stoothoff and D. Murdoch, *The Philosophical Writings of Descartes*, Vol. I (Cambridge: Cambridge University Press, 1995).

Descartes, René, *Meditations* [*Meditationes de prima philosophia*, 1641], trans. in J. Cottingham, R. Stoothoff and D. Murdoch, *The Philosophical Writings of Descartes*, Vol. II (Cambridge: Cambridge University Press, 1995).

Descartes, René, *Principles of Philosophy* [*Principia philosophiae*, 1644], trans. in J. Cottingham, R. Stoothoff and D. Murdoch, *The*

Philosophical Writings of Descartes, Vol. I (Cambridge: Cambridge University Press, 1995).

Donagan, Alan, 'Spinoza's Theology', in D. Garrett (ed.), *The Cambridge Companion to Spinoza* (Cambridge: Cambridge University Press, 1996), Ch. 8.

Frege, Gottlob, *The Basic Laws of Arithmetic* [*Die Grundgesetze der Arithmetik*, Vol. I, 1893], trans. M. Furth (Berkeley: University of California Press, 1964).

Garrett, D. (ed.), *The Cambridge Companion to Spinoza* (Cambridge: Cambridge University Press, 1996).

Hampson, Daphne, *After Christianity* (London: SCM Press, 2002).

Hedley, Douglas, *Living Forms of the Imagination* (London: T & T Clark, 2008).

Heidegger, Martin, *Being and Time* [*Sein und Zeit*, 1927], trans. J. Macquarrie and E. Robinson (New York: Harper and Row, 1962).

Hopkins, G. M., *Poems (1876–1889)*, in W. H. Gardner (ed.), *The Poems and Prose of Gerard Manley Hopkins* (Harmondsworth: Penguin, 1953).

Hume, David, *A Treatise of Human Nature* [1739–40], ed. D. F. Norton and M. J. Norton (Oxford: Oxford University Press, 2000).

Hume, David, *An Enquiry Concerning Human Understanding* [1748], ed. T. Beauchamp (Oxford: Oxford University Press, 1999).

Hume, David, *Dialogues Concerning Natural Religion* [*c.* 1755; first published posthumously, 1779], ed. H. D. Aiken (New York: Haffner, 1948).

Jung, Carl G., 'Problems of Modern Psychotherapy' [1931], in Jung, *Modern Man in Search of a Soul: Essays from the 1920s and 1930s,* trans. C. F. Baynes (London: Routledge, 1961).

Jung, Carl G., 'The Undiscovered Self (Present and Future)' ['Gegenwart und Zukunft', 1957], in *Collected Works*, ed. H. Read et al. (London: Routledge, 1953–79), Vol. 10; also in A. Storr (ed.), *Jung, Selected Writings* (London: Fontana, 1986).

Kant, Immanuel, *Critique of Practical Reason* [*Kritik der Practischen Vernunft*, 1788], trans. T. K. Abbott (London: Longmans, 1873), 6th edn, 1909.

Kant, Immanuel, *Critique of Pure Reason* [*Kritik der reinen Vernunft*, 1781/1787], trans. N. Kemp Smith (New York: Macmillan, 1929).

Kant, Immanuel, *Groundwork of the Metaphysic of Morals* [*Grundlegung zur Metaphysik der Sitten*, 1785], trans. H. J. Paton (London: Hutchinson, 1948).

Kant, Immanuel, *Kant's gesammelte Schriften*, Akademie edition, Berlin: Reimer/De Gruyter, 1900–).

Kass, L. R., *The Hungry Soul: Eating and the Perfecting of Our Nature* (New York: Macmillan, 1994).

Kenny, Anthony, *What is Faith?* (Oxford: Oxford University Press, 1992).

Locke, John, *An Essay Concerning Human Understanding* [1690], ed. P. Nidditch (Oxford: Clarendon, repr. 1984).

Lovibond, Sabina, *Ethical Formation* (Cambridge, Mass.: Harvard University Press, 2002).

MacIntyre, Alasdair, *Dependent Rational Animals* (London: Duckworth, 1999).

Mackie, John, *Ethics: Inventing Right and Wrong* (Harmondsworth: Penguin, 1977).

Mackie, John, *The Miracle of Theism* (Oxford: Clarendon, 1982).

Macquarrie, John, *Principles of Christian Theology* (1966; 2nd edn, London: SCM, 1977).

Malebranche, Nicolas, *Recherche de la Vérité* [1674], trans. T. M. Lennon and P. J. Olscamp (Cambridge: Cambridge University Press, 1997).

Marion, Jean-Luc, 'In the Name', in J. Caputo and M. Scanlon, *God, The Gift and Postmodernism* (Bloomington: Indiana University Press, 1999).

McCabe, Herbert, *Faith within Reason* (London: Continuum, 2006).

McCabe, Herbert, *God Still Matters* [2002] (London: Continuum, 2005).

McDowell, John, *Mind and World* (Cambridge Mass.: Harvard University Press, 1995).

Merton, Thomas, *Seeds of Contemplation* (Clarke: Wheathampstead, 1961).

Moore, Adrian, 'Realism and the Absolute Conception', in A. Thomas (ed.), *Bernard Williams*, pp. 24–46.

Newman, John Henry, *Sermons, Chiefly on the Theory of Religious Belief* [1826–43] (2nd edn, London: Rivington, 1844).

Newton-Smith, W. H., *The Rationality of Science* (London: Routledge, 1981).

Nietzsche, Friedrich, *Beyond Good and Evil* [*Jenseits von Gut und Böse*, 1886], trans. W. Kaufmann (New York: Random House, 1966).

Norman, Richard, 'The Varieties of Non-Religious Experience', in J. Cottingham (ed.), *The Meaning of Theism*.

Parfit, Derek, *Reasons and Persons* (Oxford: Oxford University Press, 1984; repr. 1987).

Pascal, Blaise, *Pensées* [1670], ed. L. Lafuma (Paris: Seuil, 1962). Available in English, ed. A. Krailsheimer (Harmondsworth: Penguin, 1972).

Plantinga, Alvin, and Michael Tooley, *Knowledge of God* (Oxford: Blackwell, 2008).

Plantinga, Alvin, 'Divine Action in the World: Synopsis', in *Ratio* Vol. XIX No. 4 (December 2006), pp. 495–504, repr. in Cottingham (ed.), *The Meaning of Theism*.

Plato, *Republic* [375 BC], transl. D. Lee (London: Penguin, 1987).

Ratzinger, Joseph, *Introduction to Christianity* [*Einfuhrung in das Christentum*, 1968, rev. 2000] trans. J. Forster, (San Francisco: Ignatius Press, 2000).

Rigby, Cormac, *The Lord Be With You* (Oxford: Family Publications, 2003).

Russell, Bertrand, *Problems of Philosophy* [1912] (Oxford: Oxford University Press, 1967).

Sanches, Francisco, *That Nothing is Known* [*Quod Nihil Scitur*, 1581], trans. and ed. D. Thomson and E. Limbrick (Cambridge: Cambridge University Press, 1988).

Sartre, Jean-Paul, *Being and Nothingness* [*L'Etre et le Néant*, 1943], trans. H. Barnes (London: Methuen, 1957). `

Scanlon, T. M., *What We Owe to Each Other* (Cambridge Mass.: Belknap, 1998).

Schopenhauer, Arthur, *The World and Will and Representation* [*Die Welt als Wille und Vorstellung*, 1818], trans. E. F. J. Payne (New York: Dover, 1966).

Sellars, Wilfred, 'The Myth of the Given: Three Lectures on Empiricism and the Philosophy of Mind', in *The Foundations of Science and the Concepts of Psychoanalysis, Minnesota Studies in the Philosophy of Science*, Vol. I, ed. H. Feigl and M. Scriven (Minneapolis: University of Minnesota Press, 1956).

Shafer-Landau, Russ, *Moral Realism* (Oxford: Clarendon Press, 2003).

Skorupski, John, 'Internal Reasons and the Scope of Blame', in A. Thomas (ed.), *Bernard Williams*, pp. 73–103.

Spinoza, Benedict, *Ethics* [*Ethica ordine geometrico demonstrata*, c. 1665], trans. in *The Collected Works of Spinoza*, ed. E. Curley, Vol. I (Princeton: Princeton University Press, 1985).

Spinoza, Benedict, *Tractatus Theologico-Politicus* [1670], trans. A. G. Werhnam (Oxford: Clarendon, 1958).

Sterry, Peter, *A Discourse of the Freedom of the Will* [1675], repr. in C. Taliaferro and A. J. Teply (eds), *Cambridge Platonist Spirituality*.

Stratton-Lake, P. J., *Ethical Intuitionism* (Oxford: Clarendon Press, 2002).

Strawson, Galen, *The Secret Connexion: Causation, Realism and David Hume* (Oxford: Clarendon, 1989).

Swinburne, Richard, *Faith and Reason* [1981], 2nd edn (Oxford: Clarendon Press, 2003).

Swinburne, Richard, *Was Jesus God?* (Oxford: Oxford University Press, 2008).

Taliaferro, C. and A. J. Tepley (eds), *Cambridge Platonist Spirituality* (Mahwah, NJ: Paulist Press, 2004).

Taylor, J. V., *The Christlike God* (London: SCM, 1992).

Thomas, Alan, (ed.), *Bernard Williams* (Cambridge: Cambridge University Press, 2007).

Thucydides, *History of the Peloponnesian War* [c. 415 BC], trans. R. Warner (Harmondsworth: Penguin, 1954).

Tolstoy, Leo, *Anna Karenina* [1873–7], trans. R. Pevear and L. Volokhonsky (London: Penguin, 2001).

Traherne, Thomas, *Centuries, Poems and Thanksgivings* [c. 1670], ed. H. M. Margoliouth (Oxford: Oxford University Press, 1958).

Turner, Denys, *The Darkness of God* (Cambridge: Cambridge University Press, 1995).

Wielenberg, E. J., *Value and Virtue in a Godless Universe* (Cambridge: Cambridge University Press, 2005).

Williams, Bernard, 'Deciding to Believe', in B. Williams, *Problems of the Self* (Cambridge: Cambridge University Press, 1973).

Williams, Bernard, 'Philosophy as a Humanistic Discipline' [2000], in B. Williams, *Philosophy as a Humanistic Discipline* (Princeton: Princeton University Press, 2006).

Williams, Bernard, *Ethics and the Limits of Philosophy* (London: Collins, 1985).

Williams, Bernard, *Truth and Truthfulness* (Princeton: Princeton University Press, 2002).

Wittgenstein, Ludwig, *Culture and Value* (Oxford: Blackwell, 1980).

Wittgenstein, Ludwig, *Lectures and Conversations on Aesthetics, Psychology and Religious Belief* (Oxford: Blackwell, 1966).

Wolterstorff, Nicolas, *Art in Action: Towards a Christian Aesthetic* (Grand Rapids, MI: Eerdmans, 1980).

Wright, John, *The Sceptical Realism of David Hume* (Cambridge, Cambridge University Press, 1983).

Wynn, Mark R., *Faith and Place: An Essay in Embodied Religious Epistemology* (Oxford: Oxford University Press, 2009).

Index